"Nothing stretches the imagin
Himself to us as an inheritan
heart of God, and as interces
heart onto the earth. In *Praying*
how to partner with the Lord in bringing heaven to earth. Raise your
level of expectation. God is looking for those who will stand in the
gap, repair the walls and partner with Him to make history."

Bill Johnson, Bethel Church, Redding, California; author,
*God Is Good*, *The Power That Changes the World*

"I can attest to the intercessory grace on James Goll's life and his
passion for Jesus. I have known James for over thirty years. *Praying
with God's Heart* will add needed ammunition to the prayer arsenal
to inspire effective, fervent prayer from the heart."

Mike Bickle, International House of Prayer of Kansas City

"Dr. James Goll is one of the most seasoned teachers, mentors and
instructors on the subject of prayer and intercession today. *Praying
with God's Heart* will motivate you to draw close to the heart of
God and partner with Him for Kingdom advancement. This book
will empower and motivate you to pray effectively from a place of
intimacy with God."

Dr. Patricia King, founder, Patricia King Ministries,
www.patriciaking.com

"What an excellent resource! Here is a call to prayer that understands
the prophetic, a call to intercession that understands the importance
of Israel, a call to supplication that understands the Spirit. James Goll
is one of the few leaders in the Body today who could write such a
book, let alone do it with passion, biblical grounding and balance.
This is highly recommended reading."

Dr. Michael L. Brown, author, professor, radio/TV host;
founder and president, FIRE School of Ministry

"I hear from people all the time that their prayer lives are shallow or
that they need an upgrade. Here is a tool to take you into an empowered prayer journey, something every Christian should regularly invest
time, energy and even money into. You can go from the normal to the
adventurous spiritual encounters that James Goll has in his own life.
Read this book and inherit the prayer life you have been praying for!"

Shawn Bolz, president, Bolz Ministries

"If there is anyone who knows how to pray with God's heart, it's
James. Having had the opportunity to sit, pray and prophesy with him,

I'm excited for readers who will learn from him through this book. His revelation and practical advice will revolutionize your prayer life."

Jennifer LeClaire, senior leader, Awakening House of Prayer, Ignite Prophetic Network

"Go ahead. Thank the Lord in advance for what He is going to do to your prayer life once you read this book. You will find yourself breathing in the atmosphere of the Spirit and breathing out the spirit of prayer. I certainly did!"

Laura Harris Smith, C.N.C., author, nutritionist; TV host, *theTHREE*

"James Goll is a true prophetic father who has labored for many years to see a thriving and mature prophetic people arise. In *Praying with God's Heart* James perfectly connects the dots between prayer and prophetic. Prophets and prophetic people are by nature intercessors and those who are intimate with God. This book will kick-start your prophetic prayer life and launch you into new dimensions."

Ryan LeStrange, author, *Hell's Toxic Trio*

"James Goll speaks of the kind of biblically informed intercession that transformed the age of Wesley, set ablaze the meadows of Cane Ridge and, as in Wales and at Azusa Street, shaped the course of nations. If it is true, as Jonathan Edwards said, that 'when God determines to give His people revival, He sets them a-praying,' then this book is as much a hopeful sign as it is a fresh unveiling of God's ways."

Stephen Mansfield, *New York Times* bestselling author

"If the Lord called His own house an eternal house of prayer, there must be incredible depths and dimensions of prayer we have yet to discover. One who could show us such profound and prophetic revelation would need to be a humble seeker, a desperate travailer and a warring prevailer. I know of no man more qualified to take us on that journey than James Goll."

Dr. Ché Ahn, Harvest International Ministries; HRock Church, Pasadena, California

"Devour this book! James Goll gives not just an understanding of the theology of intercession but of how the principles apply in your daily life. Through many years of prayerful living, James is able to impart these truths to others. I encourage every believer in every church to read this book."

Mahesh Chavda, All Nations Church, Charlotte, North Carolina

# PRAYING
## WITH
# *God's*
# HEART

# Books by James W. Goll

# PRAYING
WITH
*God's*
HEART

## THE **POWER** AND **PURPOSE** OF
## **PROPHETIC INTERCESSION**

## JAMES W. GOLL

**Chosen**
*a division of Baker Publishing Group*
Minneapolis, Minnesota

Revised and updated from *The Prophetic Intercessor* (2007)

Published by Chosen Books
11400 Hampshire Avenue South
Bloomington, Minnesota 55438
www.chosenbooks.com

Chosen Books is a division of
Baker Publishing Group, Grand Rapids, Michigan

Printed in the United States of America

ISBN 978-0-8007-9877-2

Library of Congress Cataloging-in-Publication Control Number: 2018019477

Cover design by Rob Williams, InsideOutCreativeArts

18   19   20   21   22   23   24        7   6   5   4   3   2   1

I dedicate this book to the memory of my dear late wife, Michal Ann Goll, to whom I had the honor of being married for more than 32 years. Though she passed through the thin veil into heaven in the fall of 2008, she yet remains a source of inspiration to many around the world. A rare example of character and gifting brought together in one person, she helped pave the way for an entire generation of prophetic intercessors to arise. She was my best friend, closest confidante and greatest support in life and ministry. I still miss her every day and just wish we could have one more prayer time together.

# Contents

# Foreword

*P*artnering in prayer with God is one of the greatest honors and privileges bestowed upon believers in Christ Jesus. Prayer changes things. Praying with God's heart moves mountains, calls forth the prophetic destiny upon a generation and brings you closer to the heart of God Himself!

Often when I arise in the morning, I go right into my prayer room. There is a little, old-fashioned couch in a corner of the room that is my "kneeling spot." I like to meet God in that quiet place. From that small spot on the floor I travel around the world praying, doing exactly what James Goll describes in this book. I am aware, however, that I am not alone in my travels in prayer. All over the world, voices are joining mine in many languages—the harmony of God's children calling out to Him in intercession.

The prayer movement grew throughout the 1980s and '90s and has now mushroomed into the 21st century. Whereas many churches did not have prayer rooms and ministries when we started teaching on intercession, they are numerous today. In fact, I know of nations that have prayer networks made up of radical, prophetic intercessors. That is why this book, *Praying with God's Heart: The Power and Purpose of Prophetic Intercession*, is of such strategic importance. It deals with the power of prophetic intercession—praying God's Word, will and ways into the earth.

While some books, like my own *Possessing the Gates of the Enemy*, touch on this subject, none covers it as well as this one. James Goll writes about intercession and prophetic intercession with humor, integrity and deep insight, plumbing deep wells of understanding from which others have given us only a light drink.

The Body of Christ needs this book. You will want to read some chapters more than once, because each time you do, you will receive fresh insight and understanding.

I invite you to take a new journey into the realm of prophetic intercession with my friend James Goll. Open the pages of this book and drink deeply of its revelation. You will come away refreshed, encouraged, challenged and nearer to God than you have ever been.

Cindy Jacobs, co-founder, Generals International

# Acknowledgments

*I* have labored over this message for years. Greater intimacy with God and the purpose and power of prophetic intercession are my primary life messages. I was born to lean my head against the chest of the Messiah like John the beloved and hear the rumblings in God's heart. I was born for prophetic intercession! I trust that this message will have an impact on you.

I want to take a moment to acknowledge two of the main intercessory tutors the Lord put into my life. Thanks to Mahesh Chavda of All Nations Church for his relentless example of prayer and fasting. You were there for Michal Ann and me to call forth healing for her barren womb. You have been there to encourage me to continue when life got rough. You remain there for me today. Thank you, Mahesh, for blessing my life and family beyond measure.

I also wish to acknowledge my dear friend of years, the founder of the International House of Prayer in Kansas City, Mike Bickle. I was blessed to serve with this passionate lover of God in Kansas City for several years. What an example you have been to thousands to keep prayer central amidst the swirl of many good things to do. Thank you, Mike, for never giving up!

I also want to acknowledge some of the others who have had an impact on my journey as an intercessor over the years: Dick Simmons, for his model of reminding God of His Word; Dutch Sheets, for his governmental warrior anointing; Cindy Jacobs, for her precision in discernment; Beth Alves, for teaching us about the "prayer shield"; Lou Engle, for his relentless pursuit of God; and Pat Gastineau, for her wisdom from the trenches.

I also want to thank all the past and present staff and board of directors of God Encounters Ministries, formerly known as Encounters Network. You have lifted up my arms to aid me in my many endeavors. You have been a source of strength and blessing in many times of need. What a treasure you are! Thank you from the bottom of my heart.

Lastly, I wish to acknowledge two highly skilled women who have assisted me over the years in my task of writing. Thanks go to Jane Campbell, editorial director of Chosen Books, and to Kathy Deering, my writing partner for many projects over many years. You both make this tedious process so much fun! You help me to b-r-e-a-t-h-e.

I am deeply indebted to each of you. Thank You, Lord, for the privilege of walking with others.

James W. Goll

# *Part 1*

# A Heart for Intercession

One of the first things the disciples of Jesus requested from their Master was that He would teach them how to pray. As it was with the first disciples, so it seems that this desire is planted in the heart of every true disciple of the Lord Jesus Christ. Whether we are new believers or older ones (like me), we want to learn how to pray—how to communicate with God in worship and supplication. Eventually, it becomes a lifestyle.

Where do we get this desire to pray for the needs of others? From Jesus Christ Himself, whose whole life consists of priestly intercession in our behalf:

> God took an oath that Christ would always be a Priest, although he never said that of other priests. Only to Christ he said, "The Lord has sworn and will never change his mind: You are a Priest forever, with the rank of Melchizedek." Because of God's oath, Christ can guarantee forever the success of this new and better arrangement.

Under the old arrangement there had to be many priests so that when the older ones died off, the system could still be carried on by others who took their places.

But Jesus lives forever and continues to be a Priest so that no one else is needed.

Hebrews 7:20–24 TLB

Jesus Himself draws us into His work of continual high-priestly prayer: "He is able also to save forever those who draw near to God through Him, since *He always lives to make intercession for them*" (Hebrews 7:25, emphasis added).

We can walk securely in our identity as His own chosen people, leaning hard on the fact that He wants the best for us:

Who will bring a charge against God's elect? God is the one who justifies; who is the one who condemns? *Christ Jesus* is He who died, yes, rather who was raised, who is at the right hand of God, *who also intercedes for us.*

Romans 8:33–34, emphasis added

We need to be reminded all the time. We so easily become self-absorbed. Distractions pull us away from the sure knowledge of our position in and with our elder Brother, Jesus Christ. We forget that we belong to Him, body, soul and spirit, and that He wants us to remain close to Him all the days of our life. Not only will He take care of our needs, He will draw us into His work of intercession.

In the first four chapters of this book, I will lay the groundwork for our understanding of intercessory prayer, in particular the vital component of intercessory prayer as an expression of the heart of God. This is what it means to have a "heart for intercession."

Later in the book, I will go into what it means to be both a priest and prophet in the Kingdom of God. Where a heart of intercession is concerned, the high priesthood of Jesus is the summation of what it means for us to serve with Him, linking the needs of earth to heavenly provision.

Embracing a heart of intercession means having a heart of compassion like His, even sometimes to the point of tears. It means holding on to hope with unshakable faith. From time to time, it means participating in dramatic breakthroughs and spiritual encounters that are almost too wonderful for words. Believe me, this is why you were born!

We have received a grand invitation to a life-altering adventure. Let's get started on our journey together—a journey into the heart of God.

# 1

# The Life of Intercession

*Invitation to Enter In*

*M*y beginnings were humble. I grew up in the tiny farming community of Cowgill, Missouri, where my family was part of the Cowgill Methodist Church. We were not well-to-do in any way except for one: a testimony of faith on my maternal side.

My mother, you see, had dedicated me to the Lord before I was born. She and my father were married at the end of World War II and they had two daughters before I came along. She was a prayer warrior and she had been praying for a son. When she miscarried a pregnancy on July 3, 1951, and found out that she had been carrying a boy, she felt she had lost her promised son, but that day she prayed and said, "Lord, if You will give me another son, I will dedicate him to Christ's service."

Guess what? A year to the day—July 3, 1952—I came out of my mama's womb. Mama's name, Amanda Elizabeth, means "grace" and "consecrated one," so I can say that by grace I came forth into consecration.

That makes my testimony a little different from other people's, but we all have to start somewhere. God calls us and we say yes. Some people can tell you the exact moment in history when that happened. For me, I simply grew up walking with Jesus as my best friend. By grace, He has been close to me every day of my conscious awareness, and I learned to both talk to Him and listen to Him from the earliest age.

## Prayer Walks and Prayer Talks

A little place like Cowgill does not have a lot going on. Consequently, I spent a lot of time as a boy entertaining myself—much of it outdoors. Our house was located right across from the railroad tracks. Even as a small child, I would go on walks along those tracks, talking to the Man Upstairs in the clouds. That is just what I did. I would talk to Him and it sure seemed that He talked back. This is when I learned to sing hymns with all my heart.

Even later in my life when I went off to college, I thought that was normal Christianity: You talk to God and He talks back to you. When He talks, you listen and respond. By then I had run into people who did not believe that, but I knew it was a real relationship with real back-and-forth communication.

Somehow, those prayer walks and prayer talks imprinted upon my heart three simple but profound prayers. I prayed them throughout my youth and I still pray them today. The three prayers are as follows:

1. "Give me wisdom beyond my years, like Solomon."
2. "Raise up modern-day Josephs with the spirit of counsel upon their lives to speak to those in authority."
3. "Give me a heart of purity and keep me from the evil way."

The Spirit of God must have given me those specific prayers, because they were far beyond my understanding. I do not think I even knew who Solomon was, to be honest, although I may have picked up his name from a Sunday school lesson.

Those prayers have lasting significance. I still pray them. I am convinced that I need that level of help more today than when I was ten years old. They are the foundational prayers of my heart to this day.

People know me as a prophetic author or speaker or as a seer, but where the prophetic waters run deepest in my life is at the convergence of the prophetic, revelatory dimensions of the Holy Spirit (from God down to earth) mixed together with prayer (from earth back to God). That is what we will be exploring together in this book.

## Starting with Worship

Besides walking and talking with God, I grew up singing to Him. I sang to Him in church, of course, practically learning the old Methodist hymnal by heart, but I also sang everywhere else. Day and night. And I sang *loudly*, to the point that some people might not have necessarily appreciated it. I worshiped in song with all of my heart.

Scripture says, "Whatever you do, do it heartily [with all your heart], as to the Lord and not to men" (Colossians 3:23 NKJV). That may be one of my life mottoes.

Worship is the act of giving ourselves to God wholeheartedly. It is about the heart. It is about giving our entire being—spirit, soul and body—to God. Twelve different Hebrew and Greek words in the Bible are translated *worship*. All four of the Hebrew words, and especially the primary word, *shachah*, mean "to depress, prostrate (in homage to royalty or God)—bow down, crouch, fall down (flat), humbly beseech, do (make) obeisance, do reverence, make to stoop, worship."[1] One Greek word for "worship" is *proskuneo*, which means: to kiss (as a dog licks his master's hand); to prostrate oneself in homage; to do reverence; to adore.[2]

In the Bible, the first mention of the word *worship* is found in Genesis 22, after the Lord asked Abraham to offer his son Isaac before Him on Mount Moriah. Abraham rose early the next morning, summoned the young men who served under him, saddled his donkey and launched out in obedience to present his son before God. After three days of travel, Abraham's eyes rested on the site of sacrifice. "Abraham said to his young men, 'Stay here with the donkey, and I and the lad will go over there; and we will *worship* and return to you'" (verse 5, emphasis added).

We often connect worship with music and sometimes make them synonymous. But there is no mention of music here. The only instruments listed are wood, fire and a knife, and I do not think Abraham had in mind to whittle a flute and play a tune. The scriptural account does not mention stringed instruments, drums or lutes. All he offered was sacrifice, obedience and faith. This is worship in its highest form—played on the instrument of a pure human heart.

Abraham is now known as a father of faith (see Hebrews 11:8–19) and he is the first person mentioned in the Bible as a prophet (see Genesis 20:7). He is also called the "friend of God" (see 2 Chronicles 20:7, Isaiah 41:8, James 2:23). He models both worship and prayer for us. I am not trying to say that worship does *not* include music and singing, because it does. But I am pointing out that true worship is heartfelt and that true prayer comes from the heart, as well.

Scripture continually emphasizes expressions of worship and prayer (see 2 Chronicles 7:14; Ezekiel 22:30; John 4:23; 1 Timothy 2:1, 8). The Bible mentions both prayer and expressions of worship as integral elements in the early Church (see Acts

13:1–3; 16:25; Philippians 4:4–6; 1 Timothy 2:1–2, 8; 2 Timothy 1:3–4; Philemon 1:4–6). Let's briefly consider three New Testament accounts of how people approached the Master. We quickly find a trend: *Worship precedes petition.*

First, in Matthew 8:2–3, we are given the account of the leper whom Jesus cleansed:

> A leper came to Him and bowed down before Him, and said, "Lord, if You are willing, You can make me clean." Jesus stretched out His hand and touched him, saying, "I am willing; be cleansed." And immediately his leprosy was cleansed.

Before the man brought forth his petition in tremendous desperation, he bowed before the Lord. No wonder the healing virtue of God came forth so quickly!

In another awesome demonstration of the mercy of God, we find prostration once again coming before petitioning. I do not believe this was just cultural protocol. I am convinced that resurrection power proceeded in response to faith, humility and true worship:

> A synagogue official came and bowed down before Him, and said, "My daughter has just died; but come and lay Your hand on her, and she will live." Jesus got up and began to follow him, and so did His disciples. . . .
>
> When Jesus came into the official's house, and saw the flute-players and the crowd in noisy disorder, He said, "Leave; for the girl has not died, but is asleep." And they began laughing at Him. But when the crowd had been sent out, He entered and took her by the hand, and the girl got up.
>
> Matthew 9:18–19, 23–25

The third example is the story of the Syrophoenician woman whose daughter was cruelly demon-possessed. The woman came to Jesus with persistence, shouting and crying out, "Have mercy on me, Lord, Son of David" (Matthew 15:22). The Lord did not answer her in response, I believe in order to test her and see how desperate she really was. Thus she continued in her urgency and would not take no for an answer:

> She came and began to bow down before Him, saying, "Lord, help me!" . . . Then Jesus said to her, "O woman, your faith is great; it shall be done for you as you wish." And her daughter was healed at once.
>
> Matthew 15:25, 28

This woman had suffered a lot, but she never lost her bearings. She surrendered herself to the Lord and would not give up. She knew where her help would come from.

When you find yourself in a desperate situation, remember how prayer works. Start by offering a sacrifice of praise. Worship your way out of a victim mindset and into the presence of the Lord. "Enter His gates with thanksgiving and His courts with praise" (Psalm 100:4).

Do not be like the people who undertake a task without putting oil on their machinery. Get the oil of His anointing from its primary source—God Himself, personally. Cultivate your relationship with Him and your faith-filled prayers will flow like streams of living water.

## Defining Intercession

Latin is one of the primary languages into which the Bible was translated hundreds of years ago, and it is from the Latin that we get the word "intercede," which comes from *inter* ("between, among") and *cedere* ("to go, to yield or to move and to pay a price")—in other words, "to go between." Someone who intercedes is an intercessor, and an intercessor goes between, steps into the gap when needed, gets involved in solving a problem. That is intercessory prayer in a nutshell.

A prayer intercessor does that in behalf of someone else, yielding him- or herself to coming alongside in prayer those who are weak or in need of assistance, standing in the gap between someone and the enemy. An intercessor moves in the direction of involvement rather than self-interest, as portrayed in the story of the Good Samaritan (see Luke 10:33).

An intercessor's heart is moved by God's heart with compassion, which makes a person willing to pay a personal price in the course of intervening in a situation.

I found a useful definition of "intercede" in the dictionary: "to act between parties with a view to reconciling differences; . . . to beg or plead in behalf of another; to mediate."[3] Is this not what Jesus has done for us? He is our model intercessor. While we were yet sinners in extreme need of redemption, Jesus Christ died for us on the cross, reconciling us to the Father.

As intercessors, we are co-laborers and partners with Jesus.

## Four Biblical Definitions of the Intercessory Task

As intercessors, we have a role to play in shaping history, and in Scripture I can see four overlapping yet distinct definitions of the task of priestly intercession.

### 1. Being a Secretary for God

Like a good secretary—or personal assistant, if you prefer—intercessors are the ones who remind the Lord of promises and appointments yet to be met and fulfilled. Why does God need reminding? Did He get amnesia all of a sudden?

No, but He has invited us to participate in the working out of His plan. He wants us to be like watchmen, as we read in the book of Isaiah:

On your walls, O Jerusalem, I have appointed watchmen; all day and all night they will never keep silent. You who remind the LORD, take no rest for yourselves; and give Him no rest until He establishes and makes Jerusalem a praise in the earth.

Isaiah 62:6–7

*An intercessor is one who reminds the Lord of promises and appointments not yet fulfilled.*

A secretary is an assistant who keeps track of the appointments on the boss's calendar. This capable assistant lays out the calendar, reminds the boss of his or her appointments and prepares the needed material so the job can be completed properly.

The intercessor, like the secretary, does the same type of work. The person of prayer searches through the divine calendar, the Bible, and finds the promises and appointments that have not yet been completed. After locating these, he reminds his Boss, the Lord of Hosts, that it is time for Him to fulfill His Word.

### 2. *Taking Up the Cause of Justice*

In addition, *an intercessor is one who takes up the cause of justice before God in behalf of another.* Here is God's perspective on the need for intercessors:

Yes, truth is lacking; and he who turns aside from evil makes himself a prey. Now the Lord saw, and it was displeasing in His sight that there was no justice. And He saw that there was no man, and was astonished that there was no one to intercede.

Isaiah 59:15–16

As intercessors, we stand in the gap before the Lord for those who are in great need or distress, lifting a cry to Him. He is looking for those who will do this vital duty. Join yourself to others in the Body of Christ who do not want to let God down. He is looking for people who will take up the cause. Injustices are rampant in people's personal lives, in their families, in our cities, in whole nations and in people groups. By linking your heart to God's heart, you can call for justice to come forth.

### 3. *Building Up the Wall*

Intercessors get to lay bricks of prayer and proclamation in order to build walls of protection around families, churches and cities. Ezekiel paints this word picture:

> O Israel, your prophets have been like foxes among ruins. You have not gone up into the breaches ["breaches in the wall," NIV], nor did you build the wall ["hedge," KJV] around the house of Israel to stand in the battle on the day of the LORD.
>
> Ezekiel 13:4–5

From this Scripture, we see that *an intercessor is one who builds up the wall of protection in a time of battle, who makes up the hedge of protection.*

The time of battle is not long ago or far distant. Today and every day is a day of battle. Satan is "like a roaring lion, seeking someone to devour" (1 Peter 5:8). Spirits of darkness want *you* for their next meal!

Ezekiel's correction was directed against the prophets of his day who were not doing their jobs, which meant the enemy could do his. Prophetic intercessors are always needed to build up the walls of protection against the enemy so that the people of God (and the Church) can stand in that day of battle.

Part of our problem is that we have not had watchmen on the walls, surveying the schemes of the devil. Satan and his cohorts have had free rein in many of our cities to do as they please. Having no guards results in no protection.

But that does not mean that things cannot change! In our day, guards, like Nehemiah and Ezra of old, are taking a stand for righteousness and rebuilding the walls of protection around our cities. This is an act of intercession. The powers of darkness are being confronted and commanded to vacate the premises they have entered deceitfully, and the rebuilt walls are being guarded once again.

### 4. *Standing in the Gap*

Ezekiel goes on to make it clear that unless God's appointed prophetic intercessors not only rebuild the walls but also stand on them as watchmen, our precious families and cities will suffer great losses:

> "I searched for a man among them who would build up the wall and stand in the gap before Me for the land, so that I would not destroy it; but I found no one. Thus I have poured out My indignation on them; I have consumed them with the fire of My wrath; their way I have brought upon their heads," declares the Lord GOD.
>
> Ezekiel 22:30–31

Look closely at this definition of prophetic prayer warriors, or you will miss its impact. Ezekiel is revealing that the prayer warrior has another distinct task: to fend off God's wrath. As intercessors, we are to take our position between God and His people and between God and the world. People of prayer are called to build up a different kind of wall here—this time the wall is between us and Him.

We are given good news, though: God is waiting for someone to persuade Him not to pour out His indignation. Perhaps the incense of our prayers (see Exodus 30:34–36; Psalm 141:2; Revelation 5:8; 8:3–5) will cause God's judgment to be averted or postponed. Our prayers can cut short, lessen or delay God's righteous judgments. We can use our intercessory capital to purchase seasons of mercy, to hold His judgments at bay. It can be like a holy wrestling match with God Himself.

Thus, here is a fourth definition of the intercessory calling: *An intercessor is one who stands in the gap between God's righteous judgments and the people's need for mercy.*

### Invitation to Join with Christ in Intercession

The Holy Spirit is looking for worshiping intercessors and interceding worshipers. We must learn both in order to be victorious.

Did you know that, when you have God's heart, you can be that man or that woman for your city, for your family, for your nation? God is not looking only for the one or two exceptionally zealous men or women out there, He is looking for His whole Bride, the Body of Christ, to respond to His invitation. He wants you and me to be His image-bearers. He wants our hearts to reflect His own. "Mercy triumphs over judgment" (James 2:13), and that is the goal of our intercession.

It is a wonderful privilege to partner with God as an intercessor. Sometimes we think of it as a difficult assignment or a spiritual discipline, but God is not our taskmaster and prayer is not really a spiritual discipline. (Which makes me think of a corrective word the Lord spoke to me once. He said, "Discipline? You don't even have enough discipline to have a spiritual discipline. They're not spiritual disciplines anyway. They are spiritual privileges.")

Our job description turns out to be one of the greatest privileges of all. You and I (and every believer in Christ) have been invited to participate in the making and writing of history. Before the throne of Almighty God, we stand as worshiping intercessors and interceding worshipers. Here's the proof:

God, who is rich in mercy, because of His great love with which He loved us, even when we were dead in trespasses, made us alive together with Christ (by grace you have been saved), and raised us up together, and made us sit together in the heavenly places in Christ Jesus.

Ephesians 2:4–6 NKJV

Therefore if you have been raised up with Christ, keep seeking the things above, where Christ is, seated at the right hand of God.

Colossians 3:1

But you will be called the priests of the LORD; you will be spoken of as ministers of our God. You will eat the wealth of nations, and in their riches you will boast.

Isaiah 61:6

You do not have to have a clerical collar to be a priest of the Lord. The well-targeted prayers of ordinary believers release glorious lightning flashes of God's glory.

After all, we are participating with Jesus Himself as we intercede. According to respected prayer teacher Wesley Duewel: "Christ is not sitting passively in blissful royal dignity, unmoved, while you intercede. No! Never! You intercede because He intercedes. The Holy Spirit conveys to you the heartbeat of Jesus."[4]

### Answering the Call

Father, in Jesus' great name, I present myself to You to be a minister and priest of prayer and worship. The goal of my life is to know God and enjoy Him forever. Now I choose to lean into Your heart and listen, to come before Your throne by entering into the intercession of Christ. Amen and Amen!

# 2

# Prayer Passion

## *Where Compassion and Passion Unite*

*A*t the end of our first year of marriage, my wife, Michal Ann, graduated from college with a degree in child development. I was already moving full steam ahead in Christian outreach ministry as a campus minister at Central Missouri State University (now University of Central Missouri). It was now time for us to consider starting our family. Little did we know the difficulties that lay ahead.

If ever I had met a woman destined to be a great mother, it was my wife. She simply wanted to love the Lord her God with all her heart, mind, soul and strength, become a godly mom and pass the heritage on. She had been reared on a farm in rural Missouri, fifteen miles from the nearest town. She thrived in that setting even though her three older siblings were all boys. She was taught the fear of the Lord at an early age from her grandparents and parents, and a dear old saint she fondly called Mr. Tyler. Her family and its nearby country Methodist church—totaling eighteen people when they all showed up—served her well. Her best friend was her Bible, and she loved spending hours with that dear companion.

She was so well prepared to be the mother of many children. Yet after we got married, the one thing she wanted the most seemed to be out of her grasp. We did everything we knew to do. Year after year we had the same results—nothing. We consulted doctors, took classes in natural family planning and received personal prayer from the spiritual Who's Who of the 1970s and '80s.

We considered adoption and applied to a Lutheran adoption agency in St. Louis. We were first on their list, and we drove across the state for a final interview. Looking around at the waiting room full of other childless couples, we could feel their pain. We excused ourselves briefly and went for a walk in the humid summer heat. Together, we offered a gift to God of the child that we could have adopted, because we felt so much compassion for the other couples. Because of God's faithfulness, we still had hope, and we did not know whether or not any of them did. So we went back into the agency and released the child that could have been ours by adoption so that someone else's dream could be fulfilled. It was a long, quiet drive home that day with both of us wondering if we had made the right decision. Yet at the same time, we had a quiet assurance that we had. Our attempts to fulfill our dream had just been exhausted, and we would need to pray our miracle child into being.

### A Promise in the Night

One night in the spring of 1980, in our little home east of Warrensburg, Missouri, I had one of those short dreams—the kind you wake up out of and remember. It was simple. The Holy

Spirit had spoken clearly to me and had said, *You will have a son and his name will be called Justin.*

When Michal Ann awakened in the morning, I shared the dream with her. God said we were going to have a son, and He even gave me his name. What could be better than that? We believed the good report, feeling total assurance that the dream was from God. A peace and gentle spirit of faith seemed to rest on us. In fact, through the revelation that came through this simple dream, we felt armed for the battle. Sure enough, we were going to have a son! After all, we carried promises of fruitfulness and healing from the written Word of God—promises like Deuteronomy 28:2, 4, 11; Psalm 103:3; Isaiah 53:4–5; and 1 Peter 2:24. We had praying people around the country standing with us. And now we had a revelatory spoken word—a three-strand cord (see Ecclesiastes 4:12). What a combination!

But circumstances did not change immediately, despite this clear little dream from heaven. In fact, circumstances continued screaming the opposite report right in our faces.

Have you ever noticed that before the light dawns in the morning, there is darkness? Well, our path got darker. Circumstances had not budged an inch. Though we believed the message of the dream, we were beginning to tire from the rollercoaster ride of hope and despair.

After a year we submitted to a long series of medical tests to determine the obstacles to achieving our goal. The further we went, the more difficult and complicated things became. Michal Ann underwent a laparoscopy and other tests, and our infertility specialist (tops in the Midwest at that time) found a condition he had never seen in any of his patients. There were multiple complications, all adding up to the diagnosis that it was not possible for us to have children.

I can still see the doctor coming out of the operating room, telling me he could not solve the problem through surgery or any other medical means. He could do no more. We had no more alternatives. We needed a creative miracle.

Well, at least now we had hard facts—detailed information—and we turned that into persistent prayer. We fought the good fight of faith, as Paul told Timothy to do (1 Timothy 1:18–19), by using the Word of God as a weapon of war. As the months unfolded we were given many valuable lessons in "Prayer 101" and we continued to trust Him who held our hands.

All the "why" questions bombarded our minds. One night, my wife told the Lord, "I won't like it, but I yield to You my right to have children."

Immediately the God of all comfort answered her: *I appreciate your attitude, but I am not requiring this of you. I say to you, you must fight for your children.*

She realized that the Lord was feeling her pain and that He longed for her to have children more than she did—and that He was pulling for her. She took a stand, saying, "From this day forward, I'll no longer blame God for my barrenness. I take the blame off God my Father and put it squarely where it belongs—on the devil!" This represented a significant breakthrough and we were filled not only with new hope but also with a courageous, fighting spirit.

In the summer of 1982 we suffered a double blow. A possible pregnancy ended in miscarriage, and Michal Ann's mother took to bed with what turned out to be her final illness. She had complete faith in God. Amazingly, although her days were numbered and her strength was fading, she had created a beautiful yellow baby blanket for the grandchild she would not live to see.

## A Touch from God

After serving as a campus minister for eight years at CMS, I assumed the senior pastor role of our small congregation,

Harvest Fellowship Church. One evening in November 1982 we were pleased to have a healing evangelist, Mahesh Chavda, visit and minister at our small church. I had met Mahesh some years before and we had become friends. He had also prayed twice for Michal Ann and me for healing from barrenness. He was especially sensitive to the moving of the Holy Spirit and was often used in the gifts of healing and working of miracles.

As the special evening service came to an end, Mahesh began to release words of knowledge for healing. He gave expression to each impression that the Holy Spirit brought to his mind. The power of the Spirit was present and people's lives were being touched. As Mahesh was approaching the close of the service, he gave out two more words of knowledge pertaining to specific healing needs. Then he gave a final word—for barren women to come forward.

The next thing we knew we were standing on the platform, next in line to be prayed for. The power of the Holy Spirit came on us, and at the same moment, we fell like timber to the floor. The presence of the Lord Jesus was so strong and tangibly powerful that we were unable to stand upright. We knew for sure that we had been touched by the living presence of our Master, Jesus.

Over the next few mornings, when Michal Ann awakened, she told me she felt warmth in her midsection. She actually felt pulling and stretching in her stomach region. It seemed as though she were coming out from under spiritual anesthesia.

Around Thanksgiving, her mother took a serious turn for the worse. For the next few weeks Michal Ann, joined by her brothers and other family members, stayed by the side of her ailing mom.

All of us gathered at her family's farmhouse for what was to be our last Christmas together. One day, my mother-in-law said something baffling. Someone in the room, she remarked, was expecting. We looked at each other. This did not make sense. No one knew what to do with the comment.

Shortly after Christmas, Michal Ann's mother graduated to heaven, leaving us heavy-hearted. Right after the funeral, Michal Ann caught the flu. Was she ever sick! I would pray for her and she got even sicker. The more I prayed, the sicker she got.

Finally one day I said to my wife, "I'm taking you to the doctor. We're going to find out what this thing is."

Off we went to the family doctor, who knew our case inside out, including the fact that Michal Ann's mom had just passed away from cancer. He did some typical tests, and then returned to the examination room.

"I have some news for you," he said soberly. "This is the kind of sickness that's not going to leave for a long time." He paused and took a deep breath. "This is the real thing."

What was he trying to say?

Then he added with a twinkle in his eye, "You're going to have a baby!" We were both elated and shocked.

It was true. On October 4, 1983, our firstborn son came into the world. As proud parents we wrapped our sweet little son in that yellow baby blanket about one year to the date it had been given to us. Holding him in that family treasure, we dedicated Justin to the Lord.

He was the first of our four children, every one of whom was prayed for passionately. As parents we learned the supernatural power of praying revelation into being as the Holy Spirit sent us the good news ahead of time. We came to know it as "prophetic intercession," and it became a vital part of our life message.

During the childbearing trials, something was imparted to Michal Ann and me. The powerful spirit of prayer was put into our souls and no one could take it away. Since then, I have known for sure that God is faithful and that He answers prayer. I am passionate about prayer!

## Prayer Passion

What do you desire? What is your passion? What do you want so badly that you can hardly live without it? James 4:2 says, "You do not have because you do not ask." This verse could easily be rendered, "You ask for nothing because you desire nothing passionately." When you want something with all your heart, you are motivated to seek it. What deep craving within you results in passionate pursuit? Do you want more of God? Do you hunger to see Him move in the earth?

Maybe we need to back up a bit and ask another simple yet profound question: What is prayer? Ultimately, prayer is nothing more than desire expressed to God. One proper definition of *intercession* is "the act of making a request to a superior." So we could say that intercessory prayer is the act of expressing a deep-seated yearning to a superior, God, asking for things to change.

The world flaunts its lustful passions daily without shame. But the Church has often seemed anemic by comparison. It is time for the Bride of Christ to be filled with passion for her Bridegroom and offer extravagant displays of love. What better place to exhibit boundless zeal and holy passion than in the place of prayer? Prayer is the bridal chamber of intimacy with our Husband.

R. A. Torrey writes, "The prayer that prevails with God is the prayer into which we put our whole soul, stretching out toward God in intense and agonizing desire. . . . If we put so little heart into our prayers, we cannot expect God to put much heart into answering them."[1]

What are some basic ingredients in the recipe for true prayer passion? Let me give you some of my thoughts, which have been shaped by the writings of the late Dr. Wesley Duewel of the One Mission Society (OMS):

1. Prayer passion incubates in a heart of love.
2. Prayer passion grows out of holy desire.

3. Prayer passion may be a special gift of God, empowering you for the precise moment He wants to use you in prayer.

4. Prayer passion often springs forth when God has opened your eyes in a new way to a particular need.

5. Prayer passion may escalate gradually from a deepening conviction of the urgency of those needs and God's willingness to meet them.

6. Prayer passion grows as you continue to give yourself to intercession.

7. Prayer passion will revitalize and strengthen your faith.

I have collected further insight from the writing of the famous revivalist of the early nineteenth century, Charles Finney, who advised, "If you find yourself drawn out in mighty prayer for certain individuals, exercised with great compassion, agonized with strong crying and tears, for a certain family or neighborhood or people, let such an influence be yielded to."[2] Finney made it clear that passionate intercession does not have to be characterized by loud, demonstrative praying, though. At times, fervent prayer may be quiet or even silent.

Although we sometimes call it "wrestling in prayer," passionate prayer is not necessarily synonymous with physical exertion. The effectiveness of our spiritual wrestling in prayer cannot be judged by our physical activity or stance. Of course, at times the use of various postures is fitting, and can help us give expression to the cries of our souls. But we do not need to work up spiritual intensity by our own human effort. Such effort does not help at all.

In any case, passionate praying does not guarantee immediate answers. God responds to many of our prayers instantly without protracted praying on our part, and many other heartfelt prayer desires are answered as you simply "delight yourself in the LORD" (Psalm 37:4).

Passionate praying does nothing to earn you better status with the Father. Fervency in passionate intercession is an out-working of the Spirit's ministry of grace within you. Prayer passion begins when you bask in the awesome love the Father has for us, His children—the supreme objects of His affection. A revelation of bridal love makes your communion more passionate than anything else.

## Expressions of the Heart beyond Words

Has your heart ever been bursting with love for the Lord Jesus, so much that words cannot express what is inside you? Sometimes when I am overwhelmed by the loveliness of His great presence, words seem inadequate. When I am captivated by the qualities of this man Christ Jesus, my heart aches and yearns with the desire to know Him and to embrace His ways. This is when prayer passion is in full bloom.

But sometimes love speaks a language that seems strange to us. First and foremost, you see, it is a language of the heart.

### The Language of Compassionate Weeping

Several Salvation Army officers in the last century asked their leader, General William Booth, "How can we save the lost?" Booth stated simply, "Try tears."[3] We do not need more church growth seminars or the latest techniques and methodologies. We collaborate with our Savior by sharing His compassionate heart, and a compassionate heart may express itself through weeping.

Twentieth-century gospel songwriter Ira Stanphill said, "My church will never grow while my eyes are dry."

Basilea Schlink, who founded the Lutheran Evangelical Sisterhood of Mary in the midst of the destruction of World War II, also knew the language of compassionate weeping. She wrote, "The first characteristic of the Kingdom of heaven is the overflowing joy that comes from contrition and repentance. . . . Tears of contrition soften even the hardest hearts."[4]

Jeremiah 9:1 records, "Oh, that my head were waters, and my eyes a fountain of tears, that I might weep day and night for the slain of the daughter of my people!" (NKJV). Jeremiah knew the power of the language of tears.

Saint Bernard of Clairvaux said, "The tears of penitents are the wine of angels."[5] One of England's most famous preachers was Charles H. Spurgeon, who wrote eloquently about weeping in passionate prayer:

> Let us learn to think of tears as liquid prayers, and of weeping as a constant dropping of importunate intercession which will wear its way right surely into the very heart of mercy, despite the stony difficulties which obstruct the way. My God, I will "weep" when I cannot plead, for Thou hearest the voice of my weeping.[6]

King David petitioned, "Be merciful to me, LORD, for I am in distress; my eyes grow weak with sorrow, my soul and body with grief" (Psalm 31:9 NIV). Again: "I am weary with my crying; my throat is dry; my eyes fail while I wait for my God" (Psalm 69:3 NKJV).

Our beloved Paul, the apostle and writer of many epistles, wrote: "For three years I did not cease to warn everyone night and day with tears" (Acts 20:31 NKJV). And, "Out of much affliction and anguish of heart I wrote to you, with many tears" (2 Corinthians 2:4 NKJV), "serving the Lord with all humility and with tears" (Acts 20:19).

Jesus Himself wept on more than one occasion. (I will pick up the story of Jesus and Lazarus later in this chapter.) At one juncture, He wept over the city of Jerusalem, His heart bursting with compassion:

> O Jerusalem, Jerusalem, the city that kills the prophets and stones those sent to her! How often I wanted to gather your

children together, just as a hen gathers her brood under her wings, and you would not have it! Behold, your house is left to you desolate; and I say to you, you will not see Me until the time comes when you say, 'Blessed is He who comes in the name of the LORD!'"

Luke 13:34–35

George Fox experienced something similar: "I saw the harvest white, and the seed of God lying thick in the ground, as ever did wheat that was sown outwardly, and none to gather it; and for this I mourned with tears."[7]

### Prayers to the Father of Compassion

The apostle Paul knew what he was talking about when he launched his second letter to the church at Corinth:

Blessed be the God and Father of our Lord Jesus Christ, the Father of mercies and God of all comfort, who comforts us in all our affliction so that we will be able to comfort those who are in any affliction with the comfort with which we ourselves are comforted by God.

2 Corinthians 1:3–4

In another letter, he urged the believers to "rejoice with those who rejoice, and weep with those who weep" (Romans 12:15).

Why are such prayers effective? Because "The sacrifices of God are a broken spirit; a broken and a contrite heart, O God, You will not despise" (Psalm 51:17).

Over and over, David poured out his heart in his psalms:

I am weary with my sighing; every night I make my bed swim, I dissolve my couch with my tears. My eye has wasted away with grief; it has become old because of all my adversaries.

Psalm 6:6–7

How long shall I take counsel in my soul, having sorrow in my heart all the day? How long will my enemy be exalted over me? Consider and answer me, O LORD my God; enlighten my eyes, or I will sleep the sleep of death, and my enemy will say, "I have overcome him," and my adversaries will rejoice when I am shaken. But I have trusted in Your lovingkindness; my heart shall rejoice in Your salvation. I will sing to the LORD, because He has dealt bountifully with me.

Psalm 13:2–6

The prophet Jeremiah poured out his heart with such passion that he was known as the "weeping prophet." His descriptions of prophetic intercession are vivid:

Their heart cried out to the Lord, "O wall of the daughter of Zion, let your tears run down like a river day and night; give yourself no relief, let your eyes have no rest. Arise, cry aloud in the night at the beginning of the night watches; pour out your heart like water before the presence of the LORD; lift up your hands to Him for the life of your little ones."

Lamentations 2:18–19

She weeps bitterly in the night and her tears are on her cheeks; she has none to comfort her.

Lamentations 1:2

Thus says the LORD, "A voice is heard in Ramah, lamentation and bitter weeping. Rachel is weeping for her children; she refuses to be comforted for her children, because they are no more." Thus says the LORD, "Restrain your voice from weeping and your eyes from tears; for your work will be rewarded," declares the LORD, "and they will return from the land of the enemy. There is hope for your future," declares the LORD, "And your children will return to their own territory."

Jeremiah 31:15–17

## A Desperate Prayer That Called Forth Life

In my own experience, I know of the healing power of hot tears. I have told the story many times about what happened to a Czech pastor named Evald Rucky whom I met on a ministry trip years ago. As the totalitarian rule of Communism was lifting, Evald ran hard and fast to keep up with the Holy Spirit in the newly opened harvest fields.

Then, on a mission trip to Sweden, he was hospitalized with a serious heart problem. He slipped into a coma and lay between life and death. His wife traveled to be by his side. His congregation, along with other believers across Czechoslovakia, kept up a prayer vigil for the now-fragile life of their beloved pastor. Evald's best friend and associate pastor, Peter, also came to Sweden to pray for him. In Peter's words, "It seemed as though I was carrying with me the prayers of the saints. I was the point of the spear and they were the shaft."

In the hospital room, Peter stood over Evald's comatose body. He had come to pray but could not compose a prayer in any natural language. So he began to weep. As his tears dropped onto his friend's body, something happened. Becoming aware that his work as a husband, father and pastor was not yet complete, Evald realized he needed to make a decision to live, and the next thing he knew, his spirit (which had entered heaven already) rejoined his body in the hospital bed. Instantly he was healed. The doctors declared it a miracle and released him without even requiring payment for any of the medical expenses!

Evald Rucky had been called from death to life through the power of compassionate weeping—passionate wordless prayer from the heart.

## The Spirit Helps Our Weakness

With this background of the language of the heart, let's consider the familiar passage of Romans 8:26–27:

> In the same way the Spirit also helps our weakness; for we do not know how to pray as we should, but the Spirit Himself intercedes for us with groanings too deep for words; and He who searches the hearts knows what the mind of the Spirit is, because He intercedes for the saints according to the will of God.

The language of prayer, you see, is a language of the heart, and the heart is not limited to the vocabulary of the mind. I have often paraphrased this passage in Romans 8 like this:

> Often we do not know what or how to pray effectively, as we should. But as we admit our limited abilities and yield to the direction of our Helper, the Holy Spirit, God will give Him the language of perfect prayer through us that is too deep for natural articulation.

This is my description of how the prayers of sighing and groaning work. And they do work!

The heart cry of the Holy Spirit is just too deep for human words. At times the depths of the Holy Spirit's prayers become groanings within our hearts that express a prayer desire so profound that it cannot be adequately expressed in man's natural language. In addition to weeping, our hearts groan with His.

In the words of Wesley Duewel from his powerful book *Mighty Prevailing Prayer*:

> Our knowledge is limited, so we do not know what is best to pray for in each situation. The Spirit's very definite and infinitely deep desire must be expressed in groanings rather than in our words, since our words are inadequate. Spirit-born groaning is always in accord with God's will. The Spirit could desire nothing other. But God can translate these groanings into His fullest understanding and do "immeasurably more than all we

ask or imagine, according to His power that is at work within us" (Ephesians 3:20).

God the Father understands the Spirit's meaning as He groans within us (Romans 8:27). Our weakness (8:26) is that our human words cannot adequately and fully articulate the depth of divine longing, just as our personality cannot experience the fullness and depth of the Spirit's longing. We can express it truly, but not totally. We are finite; He is infinite.[8]

Yes, God chooses to involve us in His intercession. He has chosen to prevail through our intense travailing. Martin Luther wrote, "Nor is prayer ever heard more abundantly than in such agony and groanings of struggling faith."[9]

Each of us has walls of resistance toward God that we neither know about nor understand how to break down on our own. Groaning is used to bring deliverance by pushing back the pressures of darkness. Groaning pushes us through tight, distressing places into the larger places of the Spirit. Groaning comes from deep within us and can be a tool preparing us for the utter abandonment that God requires.

Groaning is not for those who understand what they want to pray. It is for those who desire to reach beyond what they know or understand, the ones who "do not know how to pray as [they] should" (Romans 8:26). Those who are self-satisfied will have difficulty groaning; those who are desperate will have great difficulty *not* groaning.

Not only does the Holy Spirit have a deep love language that He will express through us, but He will arise at times with the righteous indignation of God and wage war through His people. This is the intercessory and spiritual warfare posture. Obstacles stand in the way of God's purposes, but the Holy Spirit steps up and pronounces the will of God through His yielded vessels, using a language that goes beyond natural words.

## The Prayer Passion of Jesus

The writer of Hebrews gives us a peek into the passionate prayer life of the Son of God. He penned that Jesus "offered up both prayers and supplications with loud crying and tears to the One able to save Him from death, and . . . was heard because of His piety" (Hebrews 5:7). Look at the intensity and desperation with which Jesus let His heart be known; He was not afraid to let His emotions show. "Big boys don't cry" was not true of the Son of Man!

Hebrews 7:25 goes on to show us the ongoing ministry in which Jesus engages continuously: "He always lives to make intercession for [those who draw near to God]." Amazing! For three years Jesus did miracles among His people on earth, but for hundreds and even thousands of years, He lives to make intercession. And Jesus invites us to accompany Him in His agonized prayers: "My soul is deeply grieved, to the point of death; remain here and keep watch with Me" (Matthew 26:38).

He still weeps as He did in the days He walked the roads to and from Jerusalem: "When He approached Jerusalem, He saw the city and wept over it, saying, 'If you had known in this day, even you, the things which make for peace! But now they have been hidden from your eyes'" (Luke 19:41–42).

John wrote about the emotional agonizing of Jesus when His friend Lazarus had "fallen asleep" (John 11:11). This chapter uniquely portrays the humanity of Jesus and His deep compassion.

Lazarus had a unique relationship with the Son of God: They were friends. So when he fell sick at his home in Bethany and Jesus was with His disciples, probably across the Jordan River some distance away, Mary and Martha, Lazarus' two sisters, sent word for Jesus to hurry and come to his aid. Inexplicably, the Lord waited two more days before He started to travel to Bethany. This did not make sense to the disciples, but Jesus knew from the Father that this sickness would promote the honor and glory of God and that the Son of God would be glorified through it (see verse 4).

It did not look good to anybody else, though. Lazarus died of his illness. By the time the Messiah and His disciples showed up, Lazarus had been in the tomb four days. Word of Lazarus' death had spread quickly from Bethany, which was only two miles from Jerusalem, and many Jews had gone out to Martha and Mary to console them over the death of their brother. Emotions were running high when Jesus finally arrived and was greeted by the grief-stricken Martha.

With anguish Martha cried out, "Lord, if You had been here, my brother would not have died" (John 11:21). Then she raced back to the house and called her sister, Mary, who had remained there. Now, in response to Martha, she, too, went running to meet Jesus, and the Jews who were there consoling her followed. Everyone was in turmoil; the atmosphere was full of shock and disbelief.

Upon finding Jesus, Mary threw herself to the ground at His feet. Between deep sobs she said, "Lord, if You had been here, my brother would not have died" (verse 32).

We know the final outcome. Jesus spoke with authority to the deceased, decaying body of His friend Lazarus, and he came back to life. The miracle offered undisputed evidence that Jesus is the resurrection and the life. Darkness was overcome and light prevailed.

But how did events go from chaos and uncertainty to the manifestation of the Kingdom of God? Was there a bridge between these two points?

Notice the phrase "Father, I thank You that You have heard Me" (verse 41) when Jesus prayed. He refers to a past tense prayer—something that had already taken place. Was there some act of intercession that bridged the gap between the chaos of darkness and heavenly intervention?

For a long time I could find no recorded prayer that Jesus offered up. Then I began to ponder this passage further and look more deeply into the language used.

John 11:33 begins with, "When Jesus therefore saw her weeping, and the Jews who came with her also weeping, *He was deeply moved in spirit and was troubled*" (emphasis added). The New King James Version states that "He groaned in the spirit and was troubled." According to Vine's *Expository Dictionary*, the Greek word for "groaned," *embrimaomai*, signifies "to snort with anger, as of horses."[10] *The American Heritage Dictionary* defines *snort* as "a rough, noisy sound made by breathing forcefully through the nostrils." In other words, Jesus was overcome with compassion and responded audibly with sighing, sobbing and groaning—thus interceding without words.

As you look at this story more closely, you can find at least three waves of the Spirit's presence moving upon and through the Messiah. He identified with the pain and sorrow of the people. As He did so, a wave of compassion hit Him, and He stopped, sighed, groaned and expressed His anguish to the Father.

Others, standing nearby, wanted to take Jesus to see the tomb of His friend Lazarus. As they started to direct Him there, another wave of emotion struck Him and He wept openly. He stopped, and large tears wet His face and dropped down onto His garments.

And as Jesus approached His beloved friend's place of burial, He became deeply troubled and stirred within. Like an animal snorting when it is angered, Jesus, the Son of Man, sighed repeatedly and groaned in the Spirit. Yielding to the Holy Spirit, He resorted to prayers that went beyond what Aramaic or any earthly language could articulate.

Finally, as this compassionate eruption subsided, Jesus lifted His head with confidence and said, "Father, I thank You that

You have heard Me" (John 11:41). What was the prayer the Father heard? I believe it was the passionate prayer of Jesus' heart. The Father leaned in to hear this prayer from His only Son. Even though He had not articulated His prayer in words of a human language, He had prayed in the deep language of His inner being, the place where passion and compassion come together.

As we know, the Father responded to this prayer.

## You Too Are Invited

Although to be sure Lazarus' resurrection was a unique situation, you and I and disciples everywhere have a standing invitation to enter into the intercessory ministry of Jesus Christ that extends beyond our limited knowledge. In no way will our experience ever compare to the depth of Christ's propitiatory, intercessory act on the cross, which has already been accomplished. Nonetheless, we have been invited to enter the depths of the heart of Jesus and to release sighs and groans that are too deep for a natural, human vocabulary as we let Him pray through us. All we need to do is to yield to Him.

You and I can pray out of that place of convergence of His passion and compassion. Our ever-expanding passion for Jesus and His unfailing Word mixes with a revelation of the merciful heart of the Father, and we utter prayers that rise to heaven. If He grants us the gift of tears, we weep. If the situation calls for it, we groan and sigh.

As intercessors, we do not stand before God only in our own behalf, but also in behalf of our families, neighborhoods, congregations, ministries, cities, states and provinces, and nations. We present our broken and contrite hearts to Him as our spiritual service of worship (see Romans 12) and speak out from the deep places of faith.

**Now It's Your Turn**

Lord, Your Word declares that You welcome the broken and contrite of heart. So today I present myself to You, trusting that by Your great grace, I will come in humility, leaning on You and not trusting in my own strength. Lord, unite Your true compassion and passion together in my life, even granting me the gift of tears, so that I can see life spring forth from circumstances that appear to be lifeless. Take me deeper into Your heart and let Your passion flow from Your heart to mine. Amen.

# 3

# Travail

## *The Prayer That Brings Birth*

*T*ravail? What do we mean by that word when we are talking about prophetic, intercessory prayer? My explanation comes in part from being with my wife when she gave birth, because as travail (labor) is in the natural, so it is in the spiritual.

Travail is a form of intense intercession given by the Holy Spirit whereby an individual (or even a group of people), gripped by a need and a promise that has been gestating in God's heart, labors with Him in prayer so that the new life He desires can come forth.

The definition of *travail* from *Webster's New World Dictionary* is simple: "very hard work; the pains of childbirth; intense pain; agony." I have found this definition accurate in the spiritual realm as well. Travail takes place after you have carried something in your heart for a period of time, and it comes upon you suddenly, like a woman's labor pains. First comes a nurturing of a promise; later at the strategic time that promise must be pushed forth through the "prayer canal." Eventually travail ends and you realize that the promise has been born. Needless to say, you are greatly relieved when the delivery process is over!

In my personal prayer journey, I would not have easily embraced such an arduous process if I had not been with my wife as she delivered our four children. It is hard work, particularly when things seem to get stalled. During her third delivery, when Michal Ann entered the short but painful part of labor called "transition," we thought we knew what to expect. After all, this was not our first experience with childbirth. As Michal Ann's pain level rose dramatically, I kept reassuring her, "The end is in sight!" Yet the end was not arriving. Not only was the pain intense—it was almost unbearable. Instead of continuing to make progress in the final stage of dilation, the cervical opening became smaller. The contractions, instead of pushing the baby down the birth canal, began to clamp down and enclose him. My dear wife was caught in transition for more than an hour.

Let me tell you, my own efforts were no help. I had been trying to comfort her but I did it all wrong. To my shock, she began to scream out, "I can't do it! I can't take this any longer!"

We had no choice, of course. We could not decide this late in the game not to have our baby after all. We felt we were fighting for this child's life. All we knew to do was cry out to the Lord with all our might. It was an intense battle, both physically and emotionally.

Finally, when there seemed to be no more strength left in Michal Ann, something else took over. She dilated rapidly and the transition was over in an instant. Out came our son, so fast that the doctor had to run over to the table to catch him as he emerged.

Since the natural realm is often a mirror to the spiritual, what lessons can we learn through the anguishing cry of physical travail? If travail precedes natural birth, does it precede spiritual birth as well? I believe so, and I can see it throughout biblical and Church history.

The difference between travail and weeping/groaning, described in the previous chapter, is this: With weeping and groaning, we are usually dealing with a state of distress and a judgment for sin that precipitates the prayer; we are crying out for deliverance from the present situation and we expect to see it soon, on the horizon. But the prayer of travail is God's way of creating an opening so that He can bring forth a measure of growth. If an opening was already in place, there would be no need for travail.

Just as a woman's womb is enlarged and then opened in the birth process, so travailing prayer creates an opening or a way for new life to be born. Travailing prayer comes upon us suddenly, and it leaves immediately when its purposes have been accomplished, just as we read in Scripture: "For when they shall say, Peace and safety; then sudden destruction cometh upon them, as travail upon a woman with child; and they shall not escape" (1 Thessalonians 5:3 KJV).

## Agonizing and Wrestling in Prayer

In travailing prayer, you are enabled by the Spirit of God to carry the burden and desire of the Lord, then to labor, often with pain, to create an opening and see it through to mature birth in the Spirit.

As with all effective prayer, the primary idea is to pray from your Spirit-filled heart. Different people, ministries and denominations in the Body of Christ use different terminology to describe similar experiences. Those who might not use the specific word *travail* have spoken of "agonizing and wrestling" in prayer.

Perhaps one reason that few wrestle in prayer is that few people are prepared for its strenuous demands. This kind of prayer can be physically and spiritually exhausting. You recognize what is at stake: the eternal destiny of an unsaved person, perhaps; the success of an urgent endeavor; the life of a sick individual; the honor of the name of God; the welfare of the Kingdom of God.

Wesley Duewel writes about the demands of this kind of prayer:

> Wrestling in prayer enlists all the powers of your soul, marshals your deepest holy desire, and uses all the perseverance of your holy determination. You push through a host of difficulties. You push back the heavy, threatening clouds of darkness. You reach beyond the visible and natural to the very throne of God. With all your strength and tenacity, you lay hold of God's grace and power as it becomes a passion of your soul.[1]

Do you remember the story of Jacob wrestling with the angel until he received the blessing? Let's look at that passage again:

> Jacob was left alone, and a man wrestled with him until daybreak. When he saw that he had not prevailed against him, he touched the socket of his thigh; so the socket of Jacob's thigh was dislocated while he wrestled with him. Then he said, "Let me go, for the dawn is breaking." But he said, "I will not let you go unless you bless me."
>
> Genesis 32:24–26

As Jacob found out, tenacious, persevering prayer eventually pays off. May we truly grow in the strength of the Lord to wrestle, as Jacob did, and win. Perseverance always pays off!

## Other Scriptural Accounts of Wrestling

We do not know for certain what Paul meant, but ponder the following passage from Colossians:

> Epaphras, who is one of your number, a bondslave of Jesus Christ, sends you his greetings, *always laboring earnestly for you in his prayers*, that you may stand perfect and fully assured in all the will of God. For I testify for him that *he has a deep concern for you* and for those who are in Laodicea and Hierapolis.
>
> Colossians 4:12–13, emphasis added

The New International Version says Epaphras was "always wrestling in prayer." I wonder what his "deep concern" was. Certainly it was something intense and pressing enough to require laboring prayer.

When Paul wrote that our struggle, or wrestling match, is against the forces of darkness, he had in mind the Olympic Games in ancient Greece. Each wrestler sought to throw his opponent onto the ground and to plant his foot on his opponent's neck. In the same way, we wrestle against the powers of darkness, equipped by God for the fight:

> Put on all of God's armor so that you will be able to stand safe against all strategies and tricks of Satan. For we are not fighting against people made of flesh and blood, but against persons without bodies—the evil rulers of the unseen world, those mighty satanic beings and great evil princes of darkness who rule this world; and against huge numbers of wicked spirits in the spirit world.
>
> Ephesians 6:11–12 TLB

Fighting off the grasping hands of hostile forces, we must stir ourselves to press on, to take hold of God (see Isaiah 64:7).

Let's not forget one of the clearest pictures of travailing and wrestling in prayer—that of Jesus Himself in the Garden of Gethsemane:

> He withdrew from them about a stone's throw, and He knelt down and began to pray, saying, "Father, if You are willing, remove this cup from Me; yet not My will, but Yours be done." Now an angel from heaven appeared to Him, strengthening Him. And being in agony He was praying very fervently; and His sweat became like drops of blood, falling down upon the ground.
>
> Luke 22:41–44

As the writer of the book of Hebrews remarked:

> While Christ was here on earth he pleaded with God, praying with tears and agony of soul to the only one who would save him from premature death. And God heard his prayers because of his strong desire to obey God at all times.
>
> Hebrews 5:7 TLB

One common thread runs through all such accounts of supernatural wrestling matches of prayer: Do not give up! Continue in persevering, wrestling until it is over and the Kingdom of God has prevailed decisively.

## They Cried to the Lord

E. M. Bounds, a pastor during the Civil War (who lived where I do, in Franklin, Tennessee) known for his effective prayer, wrote the following:

> The wrestling quality of importunate prayer does not spring from physical vehemence or fleshly energy. It is not an impulse of energy, not mere earnestness of soul; it is an inwrought force,

a faculty implanted and aroused by the Holy Spirit. Virtually, it is the intercession of the Holy Spirit of God in us.[2]

Leonard Ravenhill, the English evangelist and author of *Why Revival Tarries,* wrote about the steep personal cost of "praying in" the Kingdom of God: "At God's counter there are no 'sale days,' for the price of revival is ever the same—travail!"[3]

Along the same lines wrote Puritan Matthew Henry, who is best known for his Bible commentary:

> The Lord Jesus has taught us to pray, not only with, but for others; and the apostle has appointed us to make supplication for all the saints [see Ephesians 6:18] and many of his prayers in his epistles are for his friends. And we must not think that when we are in this part of prayer, we may let fall our fervency and be more indifferent because we ourselves are not immediately concerned in it; but rather, let a holy fire of love, both to God and man, here make our devotion yet more warm and lively.[4]

The legendary nineteenth-century evangelist Charles Finney wrote:

> Why does God require such prayer—such strong desires, such agonizing supplications? These strong desires mirror the strength of God's feelings. They are God's real feelings for unrepentant sinners. How strong God's desire must be for His Spirit to produce in Christians such travail—God has chosen the word to describe it—it is travail, torment of the soul.[5]

Matthew 11:12 says it this way: "The kingdom of heaven suffers violence, and the violent take it by force" (NKJV). Sounds rather intense, does it not? This kind of prayer experience seems to be ignored today, with our fast-food approach to God.

We need to be spiritual historians to search out the overlooked subject of the travailing prayer. We find the following entry in the diary of the pioneer evangelist David Brainerd in North America, dated July 21, 1744:

> In prayer, I was exceedingly enlarged and my soul was as much drawn out as ever I remember it to have been in my life or near. I was in such anguish and pleaded with so much earnestness and importunity that when I rose from my knees, I felt extremely weak and overcome—I could scarcely walk straight.
>
> My joints were as if it would dissolve . . . in my fervent supplications for the poor Indians. I knew they met together to worship demons and not God. This made me cry earnestly that God would now appear and help me. . . . My soul pleaded long.[6]

Brainerd was a pioneer, leading many Native Americans to the saving knowledge of our glorious Jesus Christ. Illustrations show him kneeling in the snow, pleading with the Lord and the Indians for their salvation. We need more such wrestling intercessors in our day!

We find unusual accounts of the prayer life of John Hyde (1865–1912), a missionary to northern India, who often went into the hills to visit friends and pray. Friends reported that it was evident that Praying Hyde, as he was known, was bowed down with intense travail of soul. He missed many meals as he holed up in his room, lying on the floor, overcome with agony, crying out to the Lord. Often as he walked and prayed, it seemed as if an inward fire were burning in his bones.

It was from this intense burden that Hyde began to petition the Lord to let him win a soul to Jesus every day that year. By year's end four hundred souls had been won to Christ through Hyde's witness. The following year John Hyde cried out before the Lord for two souls daily. Twelve months later, it was determined that some eight hundred people had responded to Christ through this prayer warrior's ministry. Even this was not enough for the man known as Praying Hyde! His desperation for souls deepened, and as a result he began to plead, "Give me four souls a day."

Hyde's strategy to win souls was not typical tent crusades or large rallies. He went for each soul individually in a unique manner. He continued in travailing prayer until he had assurance that he had first won the convert. Only then, it is said, would Hyde approach someone on the street of an Indian village. Conversation would begin under the Spirit's leadership and before long both Hyde and the sinner would kneel publicly in prayer. Immediately, Hyde would accompany this new convert to a body of water and lead him or her in water baptism.

This pattern repeated itself four times a day as Hyde's burden led him to reach out to lost men and women. Multitudes found Jesus as this humble man birthed them into the Kingdom—first through prevailing prayer.

Most serious students of classic revival have been inspired by the life of young Evan Roberts of Wales, who at age 26 spearheaded a move of the Holy Spirit that touched the entire nation. Gripped by God at the age of thirteen, he attended nightly prayer meetings for the next thirteen years, asking God for revival. His prayer was simple, but uttered with anguish: "Send the Spirit now more powerfully, for Jesus Christ's sake."

Years ago I visited Moriah Chapel, the site of Roberts's historic outpouring, on October 31, the anniversary date of the original visitation in 1904. A group of us prayed together, and at the close of the meeting, a resident of South Wales came up and showed us newspaper articles he had found that very day in the attic of his house, describing the revival activity of 1904. One lead article was highlighted with a big, bold headline: "Roberts' Soul Travails." It depicted the awesome sight of the Holy Spirit visibly taking hold of young Evan's being—in public view—as he agonized for souls to be saved.

God heard Roberts's travailing prayer. In fact, a staggering one hundred thousand converts came into the Kingdom of God in the great Welsh revival!

## Travailing Prayer in Scripture

Throughout the Bible we find strong evidence of the effectiveness of crying out and laboring in prayer. In addition to the passages I have already cited, consider the following:

> Samuel cried out to the LORD for Israel, and the LORD answered him.
>
> 1 Samuel 7:9 NKJV

> They cried out to God in the battle, and He answered their prayers because they trusted in Him.
>
> 1 Chronicles 5:20

> Now it happened in the process of time that the king of Egypt died. Then the children of Israel groaned because of the bondage, and they cried out; and their cry came up to God because of the bondage. So God heard their groaning, and God remembered His covenant with Abraham, with Isaac, and with Jacob. And God looked upon the children of Israel, and God acknowledged them.
>
> Exodus 2:23–25 NKJV

> In You our fathers trusted; they trusted and You delivered them. To You they cried out and were delivered; in You they trusted and were not disappointed.
>
> Psalm 22:4–5

> Israel was reduced to abject poverty because of the Midianites. Then at last the people of Israel began to cry out to the Lord for help.
>
> Judges 6: 6–7 TLB

Gird yourselves with sackcloth and lament, O priests; wail, O ministers of the altar! Come, spend the night in sackcloth O ministers of my God, for the grain offering and the drink offering are withheld from the house of your God. . . . Gather the elders and all the inhabitants of the land to the house of the LORD your God, and cry out to the LORD.

Joel 1:13–14

### Eight Barren Women

Travail is part of birthing in the natural as well as in prayer, but there is a kind of wrestling that often precedes the birth—the kind that faces down barrenness. The women we read about in the Bible who suffered from barrenness were desperate. They (and sometimes their husbands) prayed and agonized. And in every case, their prayers were answered with the conception and birth of a child who subsequently became a prophet or a deliverer of the nation.

Let me list these eight for you:

1. Sarah, who brought forth Isaac (see Genesis 11:30; 18:1–15; 21:1–8)

2. Rebekah, who brought forth Esau and Jacob (see Genesis 25:21–26)

3. Rachel, who brought forth Joseph and Benjamin (see Genesis 29:31; 30:1, 22–24; 35:16–18)

4. Manoah's wife, who brought forth Samson (see Judges 13:2–24)

5. Ruth, who brought forth Obed (see Ruth 4:13)

6. Hannah, who brought forth Samuel (see 1 Samuel 1:2–20)

7. Elizabeth, who brought forth John the Baptist (see Luke 1:7–13, 57)

I have listed only seven barren women, while I told you I found eight examples. Who is the eighth? Isaiah 66:8 portrays her vividly:

> Who has heard such a thing? Who has seen such things? Can a land be born in one day? Can a nation be brought forth all at once? As soon as Zion travailed, she also brought forth her sons.

*Zion* is the eighth barren woman! She will bring forth her precious fruit rapidly—as soon as she travails. I have often heard it stated that if the Church would cry out like a barren woman longing for children, then we would have revival. I believe this!

Look at how the desperation of these barren matriarchs of the Bible brought about God's promise:

Sarah, who brought forth Isaac:

> Sarai was barren; she had no child. . . . Then they [three men/ angels] said to him, "Where is Sarah your wife?" And he said, "There, in the tent." He said, "I will surely return to you at this time next year; and behold, Sarah your wife will have a son." And Sarah was listening at the tent door, which was behind him. Now Abraham and Sarah were old, advanced in age; Sarah was past childbearing. Sarah laughed to herself, saying, "After I have become old, shall I have pleasure, my lord being old also?" And the LORD said to Abraham, "Why did Sarah laugh, saying, 'Shall I indeed bear a child, when I am so old?' Is anything too difficult for the LORD? At the appointed time I will return to you, at this time next year, and Sarah will have a son."
>
> . . . Then the LORD took note of Sarah as He had said, and the LORD did for Sarah as He had promised. So Sarah conceived and bore a son to Abraham in his old age, at the appointed time of which God had spoken to him. Abraham called the name of his son who was born to him, whom Sarah bore to him, Isaac.
>
> Genesis 11:30; 18:9–14; 21:1–3

Rebekah, who brought forth Esau and Jacob:

Isaac prayed to the LORD on behalf of his wife, because she was barren; and the LORD answered him and Rebekah his wife conceived. But the children struggled together within her; and she said, "If it is so, why then am I this way?" So she went to inquire of the LORD. . . . When her days to be delivered were fulfilled, behold, there were twins in her womb.

Genesis 25:21–22, 24

Rachel, who brought forth Joseph and Benjamin:

Now the LORD saw that Leah was unloved, and He opened her womb, but Rachel was barren. . . . Then God remembered Rachel, and God gave heed to her and opened her womb. So she conceived and bore a son and said, "God has taken away my reproach." She named him Joseph.

Genesis 29:31; 30:22–24

Manoah's wife, who brought forth Samson:

There was a certain man of Zorah, of the family of the Danites, whose name was Manoah; and his wife was barren and had borne no children. Then the angel of the LORD appeared to the woman and said to her, "Behold now, you are barren and have borne no children, but you shall conceive and give birth to a son. Now therefore, be careful not to drink wine or strong drink, nor eat any unclean thing. For behold, you shall conceive and give birth to a son, and no razor shall come upon his head, for the boy shall be a Nazirite to God from the womb; and he shall begin to deliver Israel from the hands of the Philistines." Then the woman came and told her husband, saying, "A man of God came to me and his appearance was like the appearance of the angel of God, very awesome. And I did not ask him where he came from, nor did he tell me his name. . . . But he said to me, 'Behold, you shall conceive and give birth to a son, and now you shall not drink wine or strong drink nor eat any unclean thing, for the boy shall be a Nazirite to God from the womb to the day of his death.'"

Then Manoah entreated the LORD and said, "O Lord, please let the man of God whom You have sent come to us again that he may teach us what to do for the boy who is to be born." God listened to the voice of Manoah; and the angel of God came again. . . . Then Manoah said to the angel of the LORD, "Please let us detain you so that we may prepare a young goat for you." The angel of the LORD said to Manoah, "Though you detain me, I will not eat your food, but if you prepare a burnt offering, then offer it to the LORD." For Manoah did not know that he was the angel of the LORD. Manoah said to the angel of the LORD, "What is your name, so that when your words come to pass, we may honor you?" But the angel of the LORD said to him, "Why do you ask my name, seeing it is wonderful?" So Manoah took the young goat with the grain offering and offered it on the rock to the LORD, and He performed wonders while Manoah and his wife looked on. For it came about when the flame went up from the altar toward heaven, that the angel of the LORD ascended in the flame of the altar. When Manoah and his wife saw this, they fell on their faces to the ground. . . .

Then the woman gave birth to a son and named him Samson; and the child grew up and the LORD blessed him.

Judges 13:2–6, 8–9, 15–20, 24

Hannah, who brought forth Samuel:

When the day came that Elkanah sacrificed, he would give portions to Peninnah his wife and to all her sons and her daughters; but to Hannah he would give a double portion, for he loved Hannah, but the LORD had closed her womb. . . . Now Eli the priest was sitting on the seat by the doorpost of the temple of the LORD. She, greatly distressed, prayed to the LORD and wept bitterly. She made a vow and said, "O LORD of hosts, if You will indeed look on the affliction of Your

maidservant and remember me, and not forget Your maidservant, but will give Your maidservant a son, then I will give
him to the LORD all the days of his life, and a razor shall never
come on his head."

Now it came about, as she continued praying before the
LORD, that Eli was watching her mouth. As for Hannah, she
was speaking in her heart, only her lips were moving, but her
voice was not heard. So Eli thought she was drunk. Then Eli
said to her, "How long will you make yourself drunk? Put
away your wine from you." But Hannah replied, "No, my
lord, I am a woman oppressed in spirit; I have drunk neither
wine nor strong drink, but I have poured out my soul before
the LORD. Do not consider your maidservant as a worthless
woman, for I have spoken until now out of my great concern
and provocation."

Then Eli answered and said, "Go in peace; and may the God
of Israel grant your petition that you have asked of Him." She
said, "Let your maidservant find favor in your sight." So the
woman went her way and ate, and her face was no longer sad.
. . . And the LORD remembered her. It came about in due time,
after Hannah had conceived, that she gave birth to a son; and
she named him Samuel, saying, "Because I have asked him of
the LORD."

1 Samuel 1:4–5, 9–18, 19–20

Elizabeth, who brought forth John the Baptist:

But they had no child, because Elizabeth was barren, and they
were both advanced in years. . . . And the whole multitude of
the people were in prayer outside at the hour of the incense offering. And an angel of the Lord appeared to him, standing to
the right of the altar of incense. Zacharias was troubled when
he saw the angel, and fear gripped him. But the angel said to
him, "Do not be afraid, Zacharias, for your petition has been
heard, and your wife Elizabeth will bear you a son, and you will
give him the name John.

. . . Now the time had come for Elizabeth to give birth, and she gave birth to a son.

Luke 1:7, 10–13, 57

## The Prayer of Groaning

As you can see, not only is desperation an important motivation to heartfelt prayer, but the actual prayer of groaning or crying out is similar to travail. In Greek, the root word for "groan" comes from *stenos*, which means "narrow"; that word is used in Luke 13:24 and Matthew 7:13, where it is translated as "strait," or "narrow" ("the strait gate" or "the narrow gate"). The connection is easy to make between groaning or crying out and bringing life to birth through a narrow place.

In the past I did not understand the connection; I thought the Bible used figurative language. As it turns out the connection is very real, even experiential.

The best known Scripture about the prayer of groaning is this one:

> Likewise the Spirit also helps in our weaknesses. For we do not know what we should pray for as we ought, but the Spirit Himself makes intercession for us with groanings which cannot be uttered. Now He who searches the hearts knows what the mind of the Spirit is, because He makes intercession for the saints according to the will of God.
>
> Romans 8:26–27 NKJV

The Greek word for "groanings" here is *stenagmos*. The Holy Spirit, in His mighty prevailing for us, prays with unutterable inward groanings. The heart-cry of the Spirit is too deep for human words, too infinite for our limited modes of expression. God the Father understands the Spirit's meaning as He groans within us. Our "weaknesses" in the first part of verse 26 include the insufficiency of our words to adequately articulate the depths of divine longing, just as our personalities cannot experience the full depth of the Spirit's longing.

We can express it truly, but not totally. We are finite; He is infinite.

Nor do we know what is best in every circumstance. Our knowledge is limited, and we never quite know what to pray. The Spirit undertakes the task of praying. His groanings become ours, and Spirit-born groaning is always in accord with God's will. (How could the Holy Spirit pray for anything other than God's will?)

The Father hears our every groan and sigh and translates them into His fullest understanding, thus doing "immeasurably more than all we ask or imagine, according to his power that is at work within us" (Ephesians 3:20 NIV).

You can count on it: The Holy Spirit will help you pray. As you yield yourself in weakness to Him, God's grace will be multiplied to you. Scripture could not be clearer about it: "God is opposed to the proud, but gives grace to the humble" (James 4:6. See also Psalm 138:6; Proverbs 3:34; Matthew 23:12; 1 Peter 5:5).

## Exemplary Praying

There was a pastor in Portland, Maine, during the Second Great Awakening in the early nineteenth century named Edward Payson. He is remembered as "Praying Payson" because of his prodigious prayer life. When he was only 26, he wrote in his diary, "Was enabled to agonize in prayer for myself and [my] people, and to make intercession with unutterable groanings."[7] It was reported that the wooden floorboards at his bedside were worn by his calloused knees into two grooves from his rocking back and forth in prayer.

Wesley Duewel writes of early-nineteenth-century Methodist evangelist John Wesley Redfield: "It is said of Redfield that in his prayer wrestling he at times groaned as if he were dying, but such mighty groanings were then followed by tremendous spiritual transformations in lives, as people repented and confessed their sins."[8]

## The Burden of the Lord

The prophet Elijah, immediately after his spectacular victory over the prophets of Baal on Mount Carmel proceeded to the top of the mountain where the burden of the Lord came heavily upon him. Here is the story:

> Elijah said to Ahab, "Go up, eat and drink; for there is the sound of the roar of a heavy shower." So Ahab went up to eat and drink. But Elijah went up to the top of Carmel; and he crouched down on the earth and put his face between his knees. He said to his servant, "Go up now, look toward the sea." So he went up and looked and said, "There is nothing." And he said, "Go back" seven times. It came about at the seventh time, that he said, "Behold, a cloud as small as a man's hand is coming up from the sea." And he said, "Go up, say to Ahab, 'Prepare your chariot and go down, so that the heavy shower does not stop you.'" In a little while the sky grew black with clouds and wind, and there was a heavy shower. And Ahab rode and went to Jezreel. Then the hand of the LORD was on Elijah, and he girded up his loins and outran Ahab to Jezreel.
>
> 1 Kings 18:41–46

Positioned on top of the mount, Elijah knew that either God would show up again, or he would be stoned as a false prophet. He took on a posture of humility and desperation. By the leading of the Holy Spirit, he squatted on the ground in awe of the majesty of God. The burden of the Lord increased on Elijah.

The hand of the Lord settled on him as pressure seemed to build inside him; something was happening.

Overwhelmed with the transcendent majesty of God, he hid his face in his hands and pressed his head down between his knees, then issued a word to his servant: "Go up now, look toward the sea" (verse 43).

The servant got up and searched the clear blue sky over the Mediterranean Sea, but he saw nothing. Coming back to his master, I imagine that he gasped to see Elijah bent down under the burden of God. Cautiously he told Elijah that he could not see anything in the sky. The prophet exhorted him to go look again—in fact, to look seven times, if need be. Off went the servant, hoping to see a cloud rising on the horizon or some evidence of a change in the weather. Each time he returned to Elijah to bring his news, he found his master with his face still between his knees.

The servant must have wondered, *Master, what are you doing?* Nothing was happening in the sky and it seemed futile to keep looking. But each time he went forth again, all he could see was the scorching glare of the sun reflecting on the surface of the salty sea.

God's grip tightened on Elijah's heart. He appeared to be in the midst of wrestling or agonizing. He convulsed with a cry, saying, "Go look yet another time."

On the seventh time (seven is the number of completion) the servant rushed out to his viewpoint, hoping to see a change. This time as he scanned the horizon, something small caught his eye. Were his eyes playing tricks on him? He shielded his eyes from the sun and peered hard. Sure enough, a cloud had emerged—but it was only the size of a man's hand. With fire in his voice, he ran back to declare the good report to the man of God, who was in full travail on the ground.

The younger man reported: "I saw it. I saw it: A cloud the size of a man's hand!"

I imagine that perspiration drenched Elijah's brow and fire burned in his bones as the intercessory burden began to lift. Then with prophetic unction he declared, "Go tell that Ahab he had better hurry or his chariot wheels are going to get stuck in the mud! For I have heard the sound of a heavy rain" (see verses 41 and 44).

So it came about that the sky turned black with clouds and wind, and there was a downpour. Elijah's travail had brought it forth.

### Praying Promises into Being

God's message for us as intercessors is clear: Do not hold back!

Elijah did not only go out and declare all he had heard. He prayed the promise into being.

Before any event occurs, it must exist in the heart of God. Before the rain came to end the drought, Elijah heard the rain with his spiritual ears. Even today God speaks first. This creates a spark of faith within a man or woman. Remember, faith comes by "hearing . . . the word of Christ" (Romans 10:17).

There are many lessons to grasp here—but let's keep it simple. God speaks. Man hears. Faith is sparked. Man responds to the spark of faith and prays the promise into being. Tenacity and endurance are required when the desired result seems to be delayed. Even when the breakthrough begins, it takes eyes of discernment to recognize it. We are not to "[despise] the day of small things" (Zechariah 4:10), as a cloud the size of a man's hand grows and consumes the sky in a downpour of mercy, ending the drought.

As we see with Elijah and many others, travail precedes birth every time. Somebody must labor in earnest, even desperate prayer. The entire created world joins in, longing for the day when God will make everything right:

For we know that the whole creation groans and suffers the pains of childbirth together until now. And not only this, but also we ourselves, having the first fruits of the Spirit, even we ourselves groan within ourselves, waiting eagerly for our adoption as sons, the redemption of our body.

Romans 8:22–23

There is a time for silent prayers—but there is also a time for bold, assertive, costly ones. You and I are not Elijahs, but when we read about his encounters with the living God we catch a glimpse of the possibilities. We might now say: "I have kept silent for a long time, I have kept still and restrained Myself. Now like a woman in labor I will groan, I will both gasp and pant" (Isaiah 42:14).

May we be enabled to present our hearts to our loving Father and may we not draw back to the relative safety behind the battle zone, but rather align ourselves with the One who is always interceding like a mother in labor. He will never give up and that should be our battle cry as well.

## A Prayer of Yielding to the Father

Father, in Jesus' wonderful name, I present my heart to You. Create in me a greater capacity to carry Your burdens and desires. Pray through me prayers that go beyond my self-limitations. Stretch me and use me as You will. In Jesus' name, Amen.

# 4

# Praying Down Supernatural Encounters

*W*hat goes up must come back down. The law of gravity says so, and so does the Spirit of God. Years ago when I was ministering to a large group of new believers in Prague, the capital of the Czech Republic, I was concentrating on my message when suddenly, slipping in between my preaching in English and the translation into Czech, the Holy Spirit spoke to my spirit: "Have you ever considered the multidirectional dimension of prayer?"

*What? What kind of question was that?* I continued speaking, and the Spirit persisted in interrupting my thoughts. Finally, He said, "Remember, what goes up must come back down."

On the spot, I got it. It was as though years of teaching and hundreds of hours spent in the trenches of prayer instantly came together in one revelation. The activity of prayer is multidirectional because it does not go only up to heaven—once it goes up, it must come back down. Our prayers ascend like incense (see Revelation 5:8) to the throne of God and then His answers come streaming back down to us. When we cry out to the Lord for help, He hears us; divine encounters come tumbling down in response to our pleas.

Always remember—what goes up must come back down!

## Ministry at the Altar of Incense

This reminds me of another word that came to me some years ago. The Spirit spoke to me and said, "Churches have 'cry rooms' for infants, but where are the birthing rooms in churches for my intercessors?" Prophetic intercessors in particular seem to be wired to be extra-sensitive, as they often carry the burden of the Lord until it is birthed into being. Let's make room in our hearts for these extraordinary intercessors.

Things *are* changing. We are beginning to set aside times and places for intercessors to cry out to the Lord. It is an irrefutable truth that as believers in Christ, we are all priests and ministers unto the Lord, burning the incense of prayer just as we have been appointed by God to do. We are learning to keep the fire burning continually on the altar so that it will never go out.

Ministering at the altar of incense is part of our priestly service, just as it was for the father of John the Baptist, Zacharias. And just as it happened to him, so too should we expect the rising incense of our intercessory prayer to invite down remarkable encounters from the heavenly realm. Here is what happened to Zacharias:

> One day as Zacharias was going about his work in the Temple—for his division was on duty that week—the honor fell to him by lot to enter the inner sanctuary and burn incense before the Lord. Meanwhile, a great crowd stood outside in the Temple court, praying as they always did during that part of the service when the incense was being burned.

> Zacharias was in the sanctuary when suddenly an angel appeared, standing to the right of the altar of incense!
>
> Luke 1:8–11 TLB

Zacharias responded in obedience when he was chosen to minister to the Lord, and the people waited expectantly outside the sacred place. From the altar of incense, his offering of incense and prayer went up. In response, God sent an angelic visitation and a promise that Zacharias' wife, Elizabeth, who up to that point had been barren, would bear a son.

It came about just as the angel had said. Elizabeth's barrenness was healed and the prophet John the Baptist was born. This is wonderful, and not only for that couple. Think back— whenever we read in the Scriptures about barren women getting healed, they give birth to prophets or deliverers of a nation. That says to me that when the barren womb of the Bride of Christ gets healed, there will be a birthing of an entire prophetic generation.

## The First and the Second Coming of Christ

This is all the more reason to keep the incense of our prayers rising: As it was before the first coming of the Messiah, so will it be before the second. This is vital information for intercessors to know.

Forerunner intercessors paved the way for the first coming of the Messiah Jesus. Anna was joined in the Temple by Simeon the seer (see Luke 2:25–38). A generation or longer was spent in sacrificial prayer, watching and worship before the very throne room of heaven. Anna and Simeon's ministry in the Temple arose (went up) before God the Father like incense, a pleasing aroma. What came back down? God answered by sending forth His only Son; the Word became flesh and dwelt among us. This Word came forth in answer to human invitation in the miraculous form of a baby boy!

As it was before the first coming of the Messiah Jesus, so will it be before the second coming of King Jesus. Globally, a generation of passionate believers will emerge with ascending worship as the Spirit and the Bride agree together declaring, "Even so, come quickly Lord Jesus Christ" (see Revelation 22:17, 20). Remember, "What goes up must come back down"—in the form of our Savior.

## Supernatural Miracles, Today and Yesterday

Just a few years ago, a dedicated house of prayer was a rarity. Today they are found everywhere. A revolutionary movement is beginning to arise that will be a force to be reckoned with. Today we are living in days we might call the convergence of the ages, in which much is happening at the same time: the passionate desire for evangelism, missions and authentic power encounters, including the release of all of the gifts of the Spirit.

When I speak of "supernatural power encounters," I am referring to what we also call miraculous acts of faith. What do I mean, "miraculous"? One of my favorite definitions of the spiritual gift of the workings of miracles comes from the late Dick Iverson, the founder of City Bible Church in Portland, Oregon:

> A miracle is a happening or event which is supernatural; the performance of something that is against the laws of nature. A miracle could be called a supernatural phenomenon. Miracles defy reason and transcend natural laws. . . . The gift of miracles is simply the God-given ability to cooperate with God as He performs miracles. It is actually a co-action, or a joint operation; man participating with God in the performing of the impossible. It is not man performing miracles, but God performing

miracles through a cooperative act with men (I Corinthians 12:19, 28).[1]

In the New Testament, we read about some outstanding miracles that came in response to the intercession of the believers. For example, take the story of Peter when the angel set him free from "death row":

> The night before he was to be executed, he was asleep, double-chained between two soldiers with others standing guard before the prison gate, when suddenly there was a light in the cell and an angel of the Lord stood beside Peter! The angel slapped him on the side to awaken him and said, "Quick! Get up!" And the chains fell off his wrists! Then the angel told him, "Get dressed and put on your shoes." And he did. "Now put on your coat and follow me!" the angel ordered.
> So Peter left the cell, following the angel. But all the time he thought it was a dream or vision and didn't believe it was really happening. They passed the first and second cell blocks and came to the iron gate to the street, and this opened to them of its own accord! So they passed through and walked along together for a block, and then the angel left him.
> Peter finally realized what had happened! "It's really true!" he said to himself. "The Lord has sent his angel and saved me from Herod and from what the Jews were hoping to do to me!"
> After a little thought he went to the home of Mary, mother of John Mark, where many were gathered for a prayer meeting.
> He knocked at the door in the gate, and a girl named Rhoda came to open it. When she recognized Peter's voice, she was so overjoyed that she ran back inside to tell everyone that Peter was standing outside in the street. They didn't believe her. "You're out of your mind," they said. When she insisted they decided, "It must be his angel. They must have killed him."
> Meanwhile Peter continued knocking. When they finally went out and opened the door, their surprise knew no bounds. He motioned for them to quiet down and told them what had

happened and how the Lord had brought him out of jail. "Tell James and the others what happened," he said—and left for safer quarters.

Acts 12:6–17 TLB

The Church had been praying fervently for Peter. God answered their prayers miraculously—so completely that they could not even believe it. As soon as their prayers went up, they came down in the form of a miraculous deliverance from death by means of an angelic encounter.

The result was not only Peter's deliverance. We see that the faith level of the Church rose to new heights as they faithfully continued to meet together, praying and reaching out to others.

### *Praying Down Miracles Today*

Like the members of the early Church, we find it hard to believe that God will act in response to our intercession. And yet as recently as a few years ago, people who study prayer were saying that as many as 80 percent of new Christians in South Asia come to Christ as a direct result of some kind of supernatural encounter.

We hear on a regular basis about Muslims in many countries that are closed to the Gospel who receive powerful visitations from angels or Jesus, often in dreams, and who come to faith as a result. As Christians faithfully pray for people who are beyond the personal reach of most missionaries or other believers, miraculous encounters occur. At least one time it was reported to have occurred in Islam's holiest city, Mecca, after several Saudi believers conducted a prayer march around the periphery of the site of the annual Hajj pilgrimage. They were asking God to establish a church in the city and to reveal Himself to those He had chosen among the two million truth-seeking pilgrims who visit the city every year to pay homage to Allah at the holy shrine. At least two sources reported that year that Jesus appeared to a group of Nigerian Muslims, declaring that He was indeed the One they were seeking.[2]

Many Argentine church leaders say that the church growth boom in their South American country has occurred as a result of their concerted efforts in spiritual warfare prayer. For example, Eduardo Lorenzo, pastor of the Androgué Baptist Church in Androgué, Argentina, a city in the greater Buenos Aires region, says that his very small congregation began to grow rapidly immediately after church members fasted and prayed against a demonic spirit. Up to that point, most of his church members had come from outside of Androgué, and he knew of no one in the city who had been converted. That all changed after the prayer effort.[3]

For some time, the Chinese church has been growing faster than anywhere else in the world, and most observers believe that this is due to the Chinese propensity for faithful prayer— a habit formed because so many Christians grew up with no hymnals, few Bibles and much suffering.

Some years ago, when I still lived in Kansas City and intercessors were "praying through the 10/40 window" (praying together for the unreached people groups that lived between the tenth and fortieth parallels of latitude), people would gather every day to pray and fast for different nations. One Sunday afternoon I was resting at home before heading out for a special evening meeting. On the prayer list, I was supposed to pray for China that day. I was tired and it affected my ability to pray. Lying down, I whispered to God, "How can I pray for 1.2 billion people?" And the Holy Spirit immediately answered in my spirit: "Pray for laborers for China." So I uttered this feeble little prayer along these lines: "Oh God, I pray that as the Lord of the harvest, You will release laborers into China."

As it happened, that evening a lady named Jackie Pullinger from Hong Kong was ministering and Mike Bickle called me up to the platform to pray aloud for her. Jackie never draws attention to herself, but her work as an apostolic missionary has opened up a great door to the Chinese people. Praying for her that night might have been difficult if I had not heard from the Spirit earlier in the day. I prayed for her and prophesied over her, again asking God to send more laborers into the harvest of China.

### What a Wonderful World

At the age of 65, I released my first-ever professional music album, *Never Alone*. As I began the recording process, I was not satisfied with my song list. So that night when I went to bed, I told the Holy Spirit that I needed His help and inspiration. I desperately wanted to perform the right pieces of music, as I had waited all my life for this opportunity.

The next morning when I woke up I heard a familiar line of a song being sung, in a raspy voice: ". . . And I think to myself, what a wonderful world. . . ." That was it!

I was meeting later that day in the studio with my executive producer and vocal coach. I asked them, "What would you think about opening with a James Goll version of Louis Armstrong's 'What a Wonderful World'?"

This idea was met with an enthusiastic "Yes!" We did it, and it is inspiring. You see, even when I was venturing out into a new field of expression, the same Holy Spirit was eagerly waiting to participate by releasing revelation. What went up in prayer the night before came rumbling back down in the form of a song. This, too, was a supernatural encounter!

### Our Response Today

You and I can pray down supernatural encounters wherever the Lord places us. We do need to repent of our fears and prejudices against aspects of spiritual encounters that we may find hard to accept. And we need to listen to the Holy Spirit—and to each other—to see what God is up to. As broken, authentic vessels, we can make bold steps of faith. As John Wimber used to say, the word "faith" is always spelled R-I-S-K.

We can pray that the prayer movement will continue to grow and that there will be a restoration of leaders like Zacharias, who are willing to minister at the altar of prayer regardless of what God might do.

You might want to consider joining me in praying the following scriptural prayer points: (1) healing for people who are deaf, dumb and blind (both physically and spiritually); (2) deliverance for those who are demonically possessed; (3) healing for people with mental problems; (4) that the lame will be healed and the dead will be raised; (5) provision for the hungry; (6) that angels would be released in response to prayers to bring people messages from heaven; (7) that mosques would be invaded by the powerful presence of the Holy Spirit, becoming 24/7 centers of worship and prayer to the one true God 365 day a year; (8) that Jesus would grant divine visitations to the unsaved and tell them the Good News.

As we pray, let's believe that God will pour down supernatural encounters, healings and miracles as He has done in times past. Let's expect a surge of Holy Spirit activity in response to our invitational prayers. Encounters with heaven always bring glory to God. May each one of us do our part to pray them down.

## A Prayer for Supernatural Encounters Today

Jesus, I am in awe of Your mighty works recorded in Scripture and in Jewish and Church history, and I desire with all my heart to see a greater outpouring of Your love, conviction and power in this generation. In these days of harvest and revival, I thank You for the privilege of ministering at the altar of worship and prayer. Together with other intercessors, I invite You to send heavenly supernatural encounters to our homes, cities and nations for the sake of the Kingdom. Amen!

# *Part 2*

# A Heart for the Prophetic

As they reclined together around the table at the Last Supper, John the Beloved, one of the original twelve disciples of Jesus, leaned in upon the heart of the Messiah. You and I are called to do the same. This book is called *Praying with God's Heart* because the only way to really pray effectively is with God's heart. Not with our weak and vacillating hearts. Not with our insufficient and tangled minds. With God's heart, 24/7, year after year after year until our lives blend into the eternal life that Jesus has won for us.

The subtitle of this book, *The Power and Purpose of Prophetic Intercession*, links prophetic intercession to praying with God's heart, not only with the desires of His heart (His will) but also with His heart's loving motivation and the revelation He supplies to us. We need to emphasize the specific and practical aspects of the outworking of praying with God's heart, but we do not want to forget that we are talking about a Heart-to-heart way of doing life.

This second section of the book (the next four chapters) is called "A Heart for the Prophetic" because prophetic intercession is at the heart of praying with God's heart. It is not just about proper mechanics, although step-by-step procedures are important. It is also about matters of the human heart that interfere with our ability to lean into God's heart. We cannot lean on Jesus' chest in intimacy if we are striving for performance-based acceptance in our relationship with God.

If I am being honest, I must say that I started out in the Christian life without a clear understanding about this. I now realize how much I felt obligated to work for my salvation because of how *free* I felt when I realized that all I had to do was receive my salvation, and then walk it out with works that match my faith. This is called grace—amazing grace.

When I first started out, I used to think that mighty works of God were reserved for the apostles and a few others. Now I know that what God wants is not just an elite group of highly gifted prophetic people but an entire generation of faith-filled followers who will go wherever He leads them.

To display works that match my faith, therefore, I must have a heart for the prophetic. Let's explore what that means. . . .

# 5

# God's Heart

## *A Prophetic Generation*

The first prophetic word I ever heard came out of my own mouth. I really was not quite sure that I was prophesying. It was in the fall of 1972. I had a little blue book about being filled with the Holy Spirit, by Dr. Bill Bright of Campus Crusade for Christ, and I prayed for a solid year, every day, to be filled with God's Spirit. Having prayed every day like that, I should not have been surprised when it happened. Not only did I get filled—I overflowed!

Among other new experiences, I started receiving mental pictures, not understanding that they were visions. I had not had any teaching.

Then one day when I was praying, a flow of words began to come out of my mouth. I was speaking far beyond my own understanding. I said something like this:

In the last week of the last days of Jesus' earthly ministry, He visited His Father's house. The zeal of the Lord of Hosts came upon Him and He declared, "My Father's house shall be called a house of prayer for all the nations." He overturned the money-changers' tables, He set free the caged ceremonial dove, healing occurred and praise broke out among the children.

In a similar manner, in the last week of the last days of Jesus' ministry by His Spirit, He will come to visit His Father's house. Once again, He will declare, "My Father's house shall be called a house of prayer for all the nations." Cleansing shall come to God's house; the Dove of God will be set free never to be caged up again. Healing gifts will spring forth suddenly and great praise will arise from the children of God across the face of the earth.

We all start somewhere, and that is where I started with prophecy. I can say, over 45 years later, that the gift of prophecy has marked my life.

## What Is New Testament Prophecy?

Prophecy can be defined as the supernatural ability to hear the voice of God. It is the very voice of Christ speaking in and through His Church today. The word for prophecy in Hebrew connotes something that bubbles forth like a fountain or a spring. In Greek, the word means speaking for another, in particular the supernatural ability to hear the voice of God and to be told something from His mind and counsel.

Prophecy is primarily for the purpose of edifying, exhorting and comforting those whom it addresses (see 1 Corinthians 14:3). It can be expressed as either premeditated or spontaneous utterances by speaking, singing or writing; through the language of dreams and visions; as a word of counsel; through music and other art forms; or by other modes of delivery. Prophecy makes the voice of God accessible for our time.

A prophetic message is authentically prophetic only if it comes from the heart of God, magnifies the Lord Jesus Christ and challenges hearers to greater obedience to God's commands.

Two definitions of prophecy to which I have often referred are as follows: The first is from Anglican bishop David Pytches, who wrote, "The gift of prophecy is the special ability that God gives to members of the body of Christ to receive and communicate an immediate message of God to His gathered people, a group among them or any one of His people individually, through a divinely anointed utterance."[1]

In his book *The Holy Spirit Today* Dick Iverson remarks:

> The gift of prophecy is speaking under the direct supernatural influence of the Holy Spirit. It is becoming God's mouthpiece, to verbalize His words as the Spirit directs. . . . The Greek word *propheteia* means "speaking forth the mind and counsel of God." It is inseparable in its New Testament usage with the concept of direct inspiration of the Spirit. . . . Prophecy is the very voice of Christ speaking to His people.[2]

I am convinced that revelatory gifts of God are for the many, not just the few. The Lord is looking for an entire generation of passionate people (called the Church) who will walk in the spirit of wisdom and revelation in the knowledge of the Lord Jesus Christ.

What does it mean to be prophetic or part of a company of prophetic people? God wants each of us to stay so close to His heart that we can speak a relevant word to different areas of society.

There are three major areas where we exercise prophetic gifts. One is the area of church gatherings, home meetings and congregational celebrations. This is equipping the Church. The second sphere is the secular community that our lives touch and influence: the marketplace, the arts, government, athletics, the business community—or even at Starbucks. This is expanding the Kingdom. The third area is speaking prophetically back to God. This is revelatory prayer—prophetic intercession.

In other words, to be a prophetic people means building a community in love, walking under the Lordship of Jesus Christ and releasing the revelatory presence of the Holy Spirit into every area of life.

## The Priest and the Prophet

In the Old Testament, priests and prophets functioned separately. The priest was an intermediary between the people and God. He carried the concerns of the people to Him. The prophet, in essence, was gifted to stand in the presence of God and he was sent to carry God's words to the people. The priest represented the people to God while the prophet represented God to the people.

In the New Testament, the division between priest and prophet was erased because Jesus set up the priesthood of all believers (see 1 Peter 2:9) and gave them His Spirit so that people could hear from Him directly.

Now all believers can draw near to God's heart, especially in these days of greater outpouring. That is why I say we are a prophetic generation, as we seek out and take hold of our prophetic position:

> Pursue love, yet desire earnestly spiritual gifts, but especially that you may prophesy. For one who speaks in a tongue does not speak to men but to God; for no one understands, but in his spirit he speaks mysteries. But one who prophesies speaks to men for edification and exhortation and consolation. One who speaks in a tongue edifies himself; but one who prophesies edifies the church. Now I wish that you all spoke in tongues, but even more that you would prophesy; and greater is one who

prophesies than one who speaks in tongues, unless he interprets, so that the church may receive edifying.

1 Corinthians 14:1–5

I will explore this topic further in chapter 9.

## The Prophetic Cry of Moses

The pressures on Moses were tremendous as he led his complaining people to the Promised Land. His cry to the Lord is found in Numbers 11:14: "I alone am not able to carry all this people, because it is too burdensome for me."

But God had a solution to Moses' dilemma:

> Gather for Me seventy men from the elders of Israel, whom you know to be the elders of the people and their officers and bring them to the tent of meeting, and let them take their stand there with you. Then I will come down and speak with you there, and I will take of the Spirit who is upon you, and will put Him upon them; and they shall bear the burden of the people with you, so that you will not bear it all alone.

Numbers 11:16–17

So Moses went out and told the people the words of the Lord. He gathered the seventy elders and stationed them around the tent. Then the Lord came down in the cloud, took of the Spirit who was on Moses and placed Him on the seventy elders. Verse 25 tells us: "When the Spirit rested upon them, they prophesied. But they did not do it again."

What an amazing event, yet what an unfulfilling outcome! With a stroke of the Master's hand, the prophetic presence that rested on Moses was distributed among the seventy elders and they prophesied—at least that one time. Thank God this was not the final word on the matter!

But two men had remained in the camp: the name of one was Eldad, and the name of the other Medad. And the Spirit rested upon them. Now they were among those listed, but who had not gone out to the tabernacle; yet they prophesied in the camp. And a young man ran and told Moses, and said, "Eldad and Medad are prophesying in the camp."

So Joshua the son of Nun, Moses' assistant, one of his choice men, answered and said, "Moses my lord, forbid them!"

Then Moses said to him, "Are you zealous for my sake? Oh, that all the LORD's people were prophets and that the LORD would put His Spirit upon them!"

Numbers 11:26–29 NKJV

For some reason two men named Medad and Eldad were left in the camp. Apparently they did not show up at the right place the first time. Nonetheless the Spirit of God came upon them as He had upon the elders, and Eldad and Medad released the prophetic presence of God in the camp of the Israelites, where the ordinary, rank-and-file people were busy with their everyday activities.

When I envision this scene, I see two wide-eyed warriors, so hungry for the Lord's anointing that their hearts' cry was "Give us all You've got! More, Lord!" God saw their hunger and jumped at the chance to lavish His presence all over those two no-names.

There is no indication that Medad and Eldad ever quit walking in the supernatural gifts of the Spirit and prophetic revelation. Perhaps they roamed freely through the camp, laying hands on people and expressing God's mighty word, stirring up holy chaos.

Whatever they did, apparently it was a little unusual. The Israelites had not seen the Holy Spirit operate this way before. Some were probably excited. They may have been praying secretly for something like this to happen. Others were uncertain and decided to wait patiently to observe the results.

Then there were the ones, as in any group, who seldom have anything good to say and who maintain a wet-blanket ministry. Well, one such person ran and told Moses, "Eldad and Medad are prophesying in the camp" (verse 27), as if it were something terrible. In reality it represented something tremendous. All the Israelites should have been rejoicing!

Even Joshua succumbed to their wet blanket, saying, "Moses, my lord, restrain them" (verse 28). This is like people today who say, "Hey, hold on. Don't you know all things are to be done decently and in order?" They are appealing to 1 Corinthians 14:40, which reads, "Let all things be done decently and in order" (NKJV). But whose order is it supposed to be anyway—man's or God's? Jesus never told us we were to control Him and His acts. We are told that the fruit of the Spirit is to control the deeds of the flesh like lust, immorality and greed (see Galatians 5:19–21). Too often we recite 1 Corinthians 14:40 as though it says, "Let *nothing* be done so that things can be neat and orderly." But it actually says, "Let everything be done!"

I am not trying to promote anarchy, doing your own thing or distrusting leadership. But the dove of God needs to be set free from His ceremonial cage. I have heard it said that if the Holy Spirit had been removed from the early Church, 90 percent of what they did would have ceased and only 10 percent would have remained. But I believe if the Holy Spirit were taken from today's Church, 90 percent of what we do would remain and only about 10 percent would cease.

Churchmen through the ages have wanted to control the activity of the Spirit. Instead of maintaining a separation between clergy and laity, Scripture shows us that each of us is a priest to the Lord (see Isaiah 61:6; 66:21; 1 Peter 2:5, 9; Revelation 1:6). Notice what Moses said to Joshua: "Are you jealous for my sake? Would that all the LORD's people were prophets, that the LORD would put His Spirit upon them!" (Numbers 11:29).

Moses' answer revealed God's heart. Let me reiterate that the prophetic spirit is for the many, not the few. The seventy leaders at the tent prophesied only once, but God yearns for a generation of people like Medad and Eldad to arise with a continuous abiding of His prophetic presence.

Are you jealous for the Lord's sake? Do you want to see all of God's servants as Holy Spirit–inspired priests and prophets before the Lord? It is not always easy.

Two enemies of the exercise of the prophetic gift are fear and unbelief. Our natural desire is to know things ahead of time so we can control circumstances. Yet as God told a friend of mine once, "My ways are inscrutable. They are beyond understanding. If they were not, they could be surrendered to man's mind and ultimately to man's control."

In John's book of Revelation, a message was given for the church at Ephesus, where John was living. He was fully aware of the Spirit's meaning when He said, "Yet this you do have, that you hate the deeds of the Nicolaitans, which I also hate" (Revelation 2:6). Commentators say that the deeds of the Nicolaitans included the promulgation of a separation between the clergy and the laity (not that the word "laity" is used in the Bible). They created a division between those who had access to God and those who did not; classifying believers and relegating some to a second-class status. This is not the true message of Christ.

## For Our Day and Time

Since the time of the early Church, we have been living in the fulfillment of Joel's prophecy:

> It will come about after this that I will pour out My Spirit on all mankind; and your sons and daughters will prophesy, your old men will dream dreams, your young men will see visions.

Even on the male and female servants I will pour out My Spirit
in those days.

Joel 2:28–29

We are all prophets now. On the day of Pentecost, Peter took
up Joel's baton and proclaimed, "Your sons and your daughters
shall prophesy, and your young men shall see visions, and your
old men shall dream dreams" (Acts 2:17).

The promise of God's presence being poured out, Peter ex-
claimed, was to the generation of his time and to all those
who would believe throughout the ages: "For the promise is
for you and your children and for all who are far off, as many
as the Lord our God will call to Himself" (Acts 2:39). In fact,
Scripture clearly indicates that as the biblical time period called
the "last days" unfolds, more of God's prophetic anointing
will be released.

This promise will be fulfilled, I believe, in our day and time.
Let a prophetic generation arise! Dreams, visions and prophecy
will flow among the rank-and-file members of the Body of
Christ. We will see "wonders in the sky above and signs on the
earth below" (Acts 2:19). The prophetic spirit is for the many,
not only for the few.

I am convinced that consecutive waves of God's Spirit will
continue to wash over us until Christ's Church has been saturated with "a spirit of wisdom and of revelation in the knowledge of Him" (Ephesians 1:17). Our Father God will not let up
until His people are filled with the revelation of the loveliness
of His dear Son.

## Cultivating God's Revelatory Presence

You can catch a revelatory anointing by being around people
of the anointing. You become like those you hang around. So

hang out with Jesus, His Word and, whenever you can, people of the anointing.

What *is* the anointing? I use the following sentence to describe it: *The anointing is the grace of God that supernaturally enables an individual or group to do the works of Jesus by the manifest presence of the Holy Spirit operating in, on or through them.*

Author and Bible teacher R. T. Kendall demystifies this for us:

> When the anointing is working, it is as natural and easy for our gift to function as eating or talking with friends. The gift is always there but doesn't always function easily. The anointing of that gift makes it function with ease. . . . The anointing, then, is the Holy Spirit. It is really just another word for the Holy Spirit.[3]

Love the anointing! Get around it, rub yourself in it and ask God for more of it. Recognize that this "it" is not an "it" after all—it is the living presence of the person of Jesus in the power of the Holy Spirit. Let's be hungry for God's anointing!

### Opening Our Spiritual Eyes

One of my favorite passages in the New Testament is Ephesians 1:15–19. In this passage we find Paul, a father and apostle, launching a letter to the church at Ephesus:

> I too, having heard of the faith in the Lord Jesus which exists among you and your love for all the saints, do not cease giving thanks for you, while making mention of you in my prayers; that the God of our Lord Jesus Christ, the Father of glory, may give to you a spirit of wisdom and of revelation in the knowledge of Him. I pray that the eyes of your heart may be enlightened, so that you will know what is the hope of His calling, what are the riches of the glory of His inheritance in

the saints, and what is the surpassing greatness of His power toward us who believe.

There was a ten-year period of my life in which I prayed these verses devotionally every day. I still pray them regularly—at least weekly. I am not one who, by sovereign gifting, suddenly began to see visions and have spiritual dreams. These have unfolded gradually over a period of time, partially as a result of praying these verses.

We all have two sets of eyes: our two physical eyes and the eyes of our spirit. We believers need the eyes of our hearts open at all times. Let's pray, then, in the name of the Lord that they will be opened up. Let's call forth the spirit of revelation into our lives as I have been doing over these many years.

### Listening, Watching, Waiting

In our pursuit of a spirit of revelation, another important quality to cultivate is a quiet, attentive spirit.

The fast-paced, instant society of our day is diametrically opposed to the gentle, quiet spirits we need to be people of revelation. The Holy Spirit is searching eagerly for those on whose quiet hearts He can write the revelatory words of God.

Recite with me the wise words of the proverb:

> Now therefore, O sons, listen to me, for blessed are they who keep my ways. Heed instruction and be wise, and do not neglect it. Blessed is the man who listens to me, watching daily at my gates, waiting at my doorposts. For he who finds me finds life and obtains favor from the LORD. But he who sins against me injures himself; all those who hate me love death.
>
> Proverbs 8:32–36

These words are filled with life. Look at the three verbs used here: *listen, watch* and *wait.* Grasp the promises granted to those who will engage in these seemingly passive activities. It appears God uses these actions to direct us into His life.

The resulting promises:

1. You will be supernaturally blessed.
2. You will find life.
3. You will obtain favor from the Lord.

But the writer of Proverbs also includes a warning: "He who sins against me injures himself." This sounds to me like a self-inflicted wound. To sin is to miss God. If this is the case, it behooves us all the more to learn these less traveled ways of contemplative Christianity: listening, watching and waiting.

These are not hard ways. But they require a simple application of a word you will notice in the midst of many psalms: *selah*. Yes, just pause for a while. (That is probably what that Hebrew word means.) We must learn to quiet our souls before God in order to commune with Him. Remember, prayer is not just talking our heads off to God and telling Him all the things we think He has not done! Prayer is not so much something we do as Someone we are with. This requires a rare activity—actually pushing the pause button.

True prayer involves *selah*. We must pause long enough to quiet ourselves and bend our ears in His direction in order to listen. You cannot hear what another is saying if you are talking all the time. It is impossible! So pause. Wait. Rest. *Slow down.* You will be amazed how this alone will revolutionize your life, opening your spiritual eyes so that the light of revelation can come in.

### Expecting God to Move

Joshua had to learn the ways of listening, watching and waiting just as you and I do. He was the choice prophetic vessel of the Lord to lead the next generation into receiving the fulfillment of God's promises. He, too, had to learn the art of prophetic intercession.

> It came about, whenever Moses went out to the tent, that all the people would arise and stand, each at the entrance of his tent, and gaze after Moses until he entered the tent. Whenever Moses entered the tent, the pillar of cloud would descend and stand at the entrance of the tent; and the LORD would speak with Moses. When all the people saw the pillar of cloud standing at the entrance of the tent, all the people would arise and worship, each at the entrance of his tent. Thus the LORD used to speak to Moses face to face, just as a man speaks to his friend. When Moses returned to the camp, his servant Joshua, the son of Nun, a young man, would not depart from the tent.
>
> Exodus 33:8–11

Young Joshua was getting the best training anyone could ever receive. He was a doorkeeper in the house of the Lord. When Moses was no longer visible, the rest of the people apparently vacated the scene and went back to their tents and normal activities. The masses went in for the big stuff—the bells and whistles, so to speak. They were content to worship from afar and did not have the patience for the passive game of waiting around, wasting time.

But to Joshua another path had been revealed. He learned the lessons of listening, watching and waiting. How? Waiting, he would not leave the tent of meeting until Moses came out from having been in the presence of the Lord. Then, watching, Joshua was the first to see the glow on his master's face. Finally, listening, he was the first to hear the report of what had happened beyond the mystical veil. Joshua's view of waiting was different from the people's. He waited in eager anticipation. He could tell that the Lord was on the move: He was going to speak, to show Himself in some way.

What should we take away from this? The importance of *expectation*. It is what changes the waiting game into an opportunity for the spirit of revelation to be activated.

### An Opportunity Awaits You!

How badly do you want to see a prophetic Church arise? How much do you want the Church to take her rightful position in broader society? Are you willing to do the little things necessary to capture God's presence and be a person of revelation?

A test awaits us all—and an unprecedented opportunity. The world is looking for answers. But will we get off the fast production line of frantic living long enough to receive something that can be heard? God's voice rings with another sound. It is the sound of consecration. The sound of revolution. The sound of revelation.

What would it be like for people to have Holy Spirit–inspired prayers ready to present before the throne of God? How much change would happen if the Spirit of revelation were wedded with holy, persistent, believing petitions and shot like arrows heavenward?

The Holy Spirit is searching for new recruits in the army of God. The Lord has put out a big sign for us each to read: *Wanted: A Generation of Prophetic People.* Yes, such people are desired by God—searched for and desperately needed. A great hunting expedition is underway. The Hound of Heaven is on the loose, sniffing out His prey. We are the ones He is seeking with His overpowering love.

Why should we cultivate a spirit of revelation? It is not only important; it is necessary if we are to intercede effectively. How else will we know what to pray for?

Do not limit yourself to selecting promises at random from God's Word to pray back to Him. Dare to take God's revelatory presence into the marketplace and world as no generation ever has before. Sign up right now to be a Medad or Eldad for your generation. Cry out for God's prophetic presence!

## Prayer for Prophetic Increase

Father, in the mighty name of Jesus, I lift a cry to You: "More, Lord! Right here, right now!" I volunteer to help carry God's heart to a lost world. I want to receive and release prophetic impact everywhere I go. Pour out Your love and power in unprecedented ways so that Your Son, Jesus, can receive the rewards for His suffering. Raise up an entire prophetic generation! Amen.

# 6

# God's Revelatory Ways

*G*od's revelatory ways"—in this chapter I am using that phrase as an alternative to the word "prophetic." I want to cover as much ground as possible in a single chapter, with the goal of taking your hand and placing it on the latch of the window to heaven. I want to give you a basic "how to hear God" guide, even if some of it ends up being a review for you.

For starters, let's spend some time on three of the most important foundational concepts that you must have firmly under your feet before you can mount up higher. In brief, they are (1) grace, (2) purity and (3) faith. We will explore them in some depth.

## It Is All by Grace

Growing up in the church, I did not understand grace at all. Sure, I sang "Amazing Grace" as enthusiastically as anyone, but I did not know what I was singing about. You see, you can have thorough doctrinal knowledge and be able to answer all the questions correctly but that does not mean that your head knowledge has seeped down into your heart. And grace, like everything else that comes from God, is not supplied automatically or received instinctively. It is part of our love relationship with God Himself.

I remember teaching a Bible study on "righteousness" back when I was starting out in full-time ministry. In the middle of it, I knew something was wrong. It felt like I was dragging through molasses or something. I was relieved when it was over. Even though I was teaching correct doctrine, my heart carried an element of self-righteousness and it was toxic to pure teaching. I may have been saying the right words, but what was emanating from them was self-righteousness. Afterward, all I could think was "my righteousness is like filthy rags before God apart from the blood of Jesus and the grace of God."

That was the beginning of a process. Over time, my mind got renewed and my heart caught up with my mind, and then my revelation caught up with my renewed mind and the cry of my heart. I am still in the midst of the process, as we all are, but the revelation that *everything good comes by God's grace* is the one I preach now.

We cannot talk about grace without mentioning its classic definition. GRACE: God's Riches At Christ's Expense. Grace is God's mercy granted to the undeserving and the ill-deserving—and I am referring to myself and to you. Grace is the unmerited favor of God.

One of the Greek words translated as grace is *charis,* which means kindness and generosity. It also means gratitude for good gifts. (This is why we call our prayer of thanksgiving prior to a meal a "grace.") In Hebrew the terms *chen* and *ratson* are used for "grace." *Chen* means "beauty, favor, and goodwill" and *ratson* means "goodwill, favor, pleasure, acceptance." Genesis 6:8 in the King James Version reads, "Noah found grace in the eyes of the LORD." This word is translated as "favor" in the

New American Standard Bible, New International Version, and others, and as "pleasure" in the Living Bible.

Grace is the supernatural enablement of God to be all that He has called you to do and to be, and you can never earn it. Many Scriptures attest to this truth:

> For we are His workmanship, created in Christ Jesus for good works, which God prepared beforehand so that we would walk in them.
>
> Ephesians 2:10

> And now, through Christ, all the kindness of God has been poured out upon us undeserving sinners; and now he is sending us out around the world to tell all people everywhere the great things God has done for them, so that they, too, will believe and obey him. . . . For because of our faith, he has brought us into this place of highest privilege where we now stand, and we confidently and joyfully look forward to actually becoming all that God has had in mind for us to be. . . . The God of peace will soon crush Satan under your feet. The blessings from our Lord Jesus Christ be upon you.
>
> Romans 1:5; 5:2; 16:20 TLB

> Therefore let us draw near with confidence to the throne of grace, so that we may receive mercy and find grace to help in time of need.
>
> Hebrews 4:16

The word *grace* is used 150 times in the New Testament, mainly in the epistles, most of which begin with a salutation about grace: "Grace and peace be unto you. . . ." That indicates that nobody is going to be able to understand the epistle unless God's grace opens the Word in a revelatory way. In reality, grace opens up the Bible to our minds and hearts, because grace opens the door to revelation.

Remembering that one of the definitions of the Hebrew word for grace is "beauty," we must recognize that the grace of God is always attractive. A person or a congregation walking in grace will therefore be attractive. But a person or a congregation *not* walking in grace will fall short. It is quite possible to preach God's light and truth without winning anyone to the message; a legalistic gospel is lifeless and unattractive.

To God, each one of us is attractive. Our beauty is in the eye of our Beholder. He extends to us His grace and unmerited favor in order to restore us to Himself—and if we walk in that grace, it should make us attractive to others. It should also give us great internal peace. Peace comes from grace. ("Grace and peace be unto you. . . .") Once you receive God's grace, your striving ceases and you no longer need to try to earn anything. You can rest in the grace and peace of the Lord.

### How to Receive Grace

God adorns His Bride with jewels of grace in the form of spiritual gifts. I cannot enter into an in-depth discussion of spiritual gifts in this chapter, but if you want more information, please consult my book called *Releasing Spiritual Gifts Today*.[1] Receiving and using spiritual gifts from God is both a means of sharing God's grace with others and receiving more grace.

When you are in His presence, you receive His grace. In the terms of the biblical blessing: "The LORD bless you, and keep you; the LORD make His face shine on you, and be gracious to you; the LORD lift up His countenance on you, and give you peace" (Numbers 6:24–26). Before and after the word "gracious" is the word "face." Being in His presence means being before His face. To impart God's blessing, you can declare this benediction over your life and pronounce it over your family and those around you.

How does this work? Just relax and receive. Stop striving, because it will do more harm than good. Whatever you earn is going to be dead. Remember, "The wages of sin is death" (Romans 6:23). You can never earn God's favor or true righteousness. Instead of trying, exercise your faith to receive. This is the truth:

> Now to the one who works, his wage is not credited as a favor, but as what is due. But to the one who does not work, but believes in Him who justifies the ungodly, his faith is credited as righteousness.
>
> Romans 4:4–5

> For by grace you have been saved through faith; and that not of yourselves, it is the gift of God; not as a result of works, so that no one may boast.
>
> Ephesians 2:8–9

Humble yourself before God—and other people. For God opposes the proud, but gives grace to those who are humble (see James 4:6–7; 1 Peter 5:5–6; Proverbs 3:34). When you are empty and humble, you can receive Christ Jesus, in whom all grace dwells. The more of Jesus' Spirit that is in you, the more grace you will have for every situation. "For of His fullness we have all received, and grace upon grace" (John 1:16. See also John 1:12, 17.)

## The Necessity of Purity

In His Sermon on the Mount, Jesus said, "Blessed are the pure in heart, for they shall see God" (Matthew 5:8). Did you catch that? The way to see God's face is to cultivate a pure heart. These words of Jesus hold a key to increasing the revelation because purity opens the way for visions, dreams, visitations and much more. We cannot earn spiritual gifts or empowering manifestations of the Spirit, but we can cooperate with God's Kingdom ways.

According to Psalm 24:3–4, you may "ascend into the hill of the LORD" if and when you have "clean hands and a pure heart." We often look at that verse in a negative light, thinking about our lists of dos and don'ts. I prefer to look at it as a wonderful invitation to ascend the hill of the Lord, to come up higher. It is a word of encouragement from God Himself!

It is not as if you can get those clean hands on your own, though. As I have been saying, clean hands come from a pure heart and a pure heart comes from the work of grace in your life. You receive His grace, which achieves an inward work in your heart. Then the external work of your hands will be acceptable and pure to the Master. It is cooperating with the inward cleansing and healing work of the Holy Spirit in your heart that ultimately produces the external fruit of greater works of your hands.

Purity of heart is like a magnet for God's grace; it draws the Holy Spirit. But we must always remember that purity of heart comes by the grace of God, lest our attempts to achieve holiness and purity of heart turn out to be dead religious works.

Purity matters, but it is all by grace.

## Faith Matters!

Purity matters and so does faith.

Faith is the constant, abiding trust in something. True faith is the constant, abiding trust in God Himself. By that we mean faith toward God, not faith in our feelings, our circumstances or other people, even leaders. True faith is in the present tense as distinguished from hope, which is future-oriented. Faith comes after repentance and is of the heart, not of the mind.

Some of us are able to believe wholeheartedly more readily than others. I have been through some major disappointments in my life and I have had to bring those disappointments to God so that He could readjust and refresh my faith. I am sure I am not alone. I have come to this conclusion: I am not going to lower the bar of my expectation or faith just because of my present (temporary, difficult) circumstances. By the grace of God, I am going to keep growing in faith as long as I live. Faith comes and keeps on coming.

Faith in God gives us the ability to believe His Word and to appropriate it into our lives. The importance of faith can be seen in the fact that it is impossible to please God without it. As the author of Hebrews wrote: "Without faith it is impossible to please Him, for he who comes to God must believe that He is and that He is a rewarder of those who seek Him" (Hebrews 11:6).

We can believe and have faith in God because of who He is. Not only is God's Word true, but also God Himself is trustworthy. He cannot lie. When we put our whole trust in Him, we will not be disappointed. Faith makes a difference in our confidence to be able to receive and gain access to the revelatory ways of God.

Our primary Scripture about faith is, of course, this one, presented here in several different versions for more clarity and impact:

> Now faith is the assurance of things hoped for, the conviction of things not seen.
>
> Hebrews 11:1 NASB

> Now faith is confidence in what we hope for and assurance about what we do not see.
>
> NIV

What is faith? It is the confident assurance that something we want is going to happen. It is the certainty that what we hope for is waiting for us, even though we cannot see it up ahead.

TLB

Faith is a present reality. Faith is a certainty. "Conviction" means it is proof of evidence, whether the evidence can be seen or not at the present moment.

How can we have much certainty in such an uncertain world? How can we live in a present reality of certainty while human-kind exercises free will? We can have certainty because of faith. Faith itself is the certainty. Faith is my anchor even though my boat does rock and toss on the waves of this stormy world.

Faith is so sure because it is based upon the Word of God. Consequently, our faith comes by hearing the message of the Word, the message of Christ Jesus Himself. "So then faith comes by hearing, and hearing by the word of God" (Romans 10:17 NKJV).

Nothing—*nothing*—is more absolutely certain than the Word of God:

Yet, with respect to the promise of God, he [Abraham] did not waver in unbelief but grew strong in faith, giving glory to God, and being fully assured that what God had promised, He was able also to perform.

Romans 4:20–21

If they violate My statutes and do not keep My commandments, then I will punish their transgression with the rod and their iniquity with stripes.

Psalm 89:31–32

So will My word be which goes forth from My mouth; it will not return to Me empty, without accomplishing what I desire, and without succeeding in the matter for which I sent it.

Isaiah 55:11

God is not human, that he should lie, not a human being, that he should change his mind. Does he speak and then not act? Does he promise and not fulfill?

Numbers 23:19 NIV

## The Mechanics of Receiving Revelation

I have been laying a foundation for our discussion of how to receive the revelatory word of God. Now it is time to talk about the actual mechanics of receiving revelation from God. Yes, I used the word "mechanics." We need to learn about the levels of revelation that are achievable, and also about the mechanics— the procedures, steps and protocols—for laying hold of it.[2]

To begin with, we must become aware of the different levels of gifting within the Body of Christ. By that I do not mean that one person is better than another, simply that there are differing levels of anointing, influence and authority. Not only are there differing levels of what you might call "gift packages," but also there are different positions or functions within the Body that require different gifts.

It is not that you need to find your identity in your giftedness or position. Even the apostle Paul never referred to himself as the Apostle Paul. He was confident in his role as a bond servant and friend of Jesus Christ who happened to be called to do many wonderful things. With Daniel, he could say: "The people that do know their God shall be strong, and do exploits" (Daniel 11:32 KJV). (That line is like an open invitation, by the way. If you cultivate hunger for God and His Word, you will come to really know Him, and that results in supernatural exploits of all kinds!)

### Forms of Revelation

One of the primary ways that the Holy Spirit releases revelation is by illuminating the written Word of God. This proves to be true for everyone, regardless of station in life or role in the Church. The Spirit breathes on the written word (*logos*) and brings it to life for you, making it into a personal spoken word (*rhema*). This makes memorizing Scripture invaluable. If you have stored up the words of Scripture in your mind and heart, the breath of God's Spirit has something to blow upon!

In my experience, one of the first prophetic operations that I undertook consistently was the ability to identify words of Scripture for people. With the eyes of my spirit, I would see Scriptures that God wanted me to tell to people, sometimes as if they had been imprinted across their foreheads or eyes. Compared to delivering accurate words of knowledge, that operation may seem like a lesser level of prophetic gifting, but people found it to be powerful and unforgettable. Sometimes the passage I would identify was the person's "life verse." Often I would not know if the chapter and verse numbers matched the Bible. I would have to open to, say, Isaiah 66—just hoping that there are at least 66 chapters in Isaiah. I do remember once getting "Acts 29" and I knew that the book of Acts had only 28 chapters. Then I got the sudden revelation that God wanted the person to move out and *live* Acts 29.

Some people enter into the "feeling" realm of revelatory gifting. They may feel a specific pain that does not belong to them, such as knee pain or pain behind the eyes. Then they need further revelation from the Spirit regarding what to do with this information. Does it apply to someone in the room? Does God want to heal the pain? These revelatory words of knowledge are an invitation to both the one ministering and to the one who has the physical need.

In addition, others receive what you can only call "gut feelings." They just know that something is true or not, or about to happen. This person will be extra-sensitive, often someone who gets touched more deeply by the feelings and infirmities of those around him or her, or even by the atmosphere of a geographic region. This is an example of Hebrews 5:14 in action—the mature learning by practice to exercise their senses to discern good and evil.

Then there are various categories of visions, anything from lights or colors or flames of fire to full visions that look like detailed pictures or develop video-fashion. Visions can occur in broad daylight or during sleep, although it may take the visionary person some time to figure out that they are not merely intense dreams.

Some revelation is not as much visual as it is audible. In a dream, for example, you may "hear" the voice of someone who is dear to you. Because you trust the voice, you will more readily embrace the message. Other times, you may think you hear your doorbell or phone ring, only to find out that nobody is there. God may be trying to get your attention. Or, as happened to me recently, you may hear specific music in a dream or lyrics may start running through your mind.

Seeing, hearing, feeling, knowing; the Holy Spirit wants to anoint all of our natural senses so we can grow in the revelatory ways of God. (For more on this theme see my book, *The Discerner*, in which I give a thorough teaching on the subject.)

Angels may bring you a message. It does not have to be like the angel Gabriel announcing the birth of Jesus to Mary. An angel may appear to you when your eyes are either open or closed, in dreams or in actuality. They may be standing behind you while you are unaware, and others may see them. Angels may not only be seen, but also felt, heard or simply acknowledged and welcomed by faith. They come to communicate divine information and spiritual revelation. More than we may realize, God sends His messages via His messengers, the angels.

Another way we can receive information from heaven is through gifts of the Holy Spirit such as words of knowledge and discerning of spirits. Often words from God come packaged within symbolic language or images. The Spirit will help you understand your own "spiritual alphabet" over time. Once, for example, I was praying with someone and I saw an image of an old brand of vacuum cleaner, a Regina, a good, royal name. I was given further revelation as to the meaning of my little vision so that I could state to the person: "Oh, God is going to do a clean sweep in your life." Even more amazing, "Regina" was the actual name of the person!

God is the Creator and He is an endlessly creative communicator. Our part is to learn to be willing recipients of His messages and to become trustworthy messengers ourselves.

### Avoiding Pitfalls

Do not worry about being a "false prophet," although Satan may try to harass you with such an accusation. "But," you may object, "false prophets in the Bible were supposed to get stoned to death! Just look at Deuteronomy 13." Yes, that is what it says. But false prophets are evil, deceived people—not simply those who "miss it" every now and then.

Just be sure to stick to the bare-bones message. There is no need to add "Hamburger Helper" to what starts out as an authentic, God-given revelation. Because it just does not seem like quite enough, the temptation is to elaborate out of our human emotions, concerns, sympathies or desires.

If you feel you must add something, be honest about it. Tell the person you are sharing with that you are about to share your own thoughts, concerns, burdens or counsel. Differentiate between words of prophecy that come straight from God and words of interpretation that are filtered through your own understanding. As you minister prophetically, learn to follow the leadings of the Spirit from start to finish.

Avoid stating the obvious, predicting developments that are likely to occur anyway. For instance, most married couples can have children if they want to. When you "prophesy" that they are going to have children, possibly of one gender or another, you may put undue pressure on them to do something for which they are not ready or that is not in God's will. It is far better to encourage people to hear God for themselves—and that includes you yourself. Learn to hear God for your own needs and to tell the difference between His voice and the additions from your own desires or others.

Certainly there are occasions when a mature prophet may predict such things, but most of us can leave such words for special situations. Our aim should be to deliver "a more sure word of prophecy" (see 2 Peter 1:19) and always to edify and promote love with our words, as Paul exhorted us:

> Let no unwholesome word proceed from your mouth, but only such a word as is good for edification according to the need of the moment, so that it will give grace to those who hear.
>
> Ephesians 4:29

While we are talking about prophetic pitfalls, I do not want to forget to mention this one: critical words, whether "prophetic" or not. Not expressing criticism is one way to keep your mind and heart attitude clean and untainted. You do not need to listen to criticism, either.

Once years ago somebody told me a bad report about a particular prophetic stream and then I got introduced to someone who was part of that scene. Innocently, I asked, "Oh, what prophetic background do you have?" and he told me. Thoughtlessly, I blurted out, "Oh, I've heard bad things about that!" That was not a good way to start a relationship. I did not really know a thing about those people, but somehow I felt I could categorize them. Thank God, my new acquaintance and I worked it out and have become good friends since then, but it does not always work out that way.

Besides polluting your mind and heart, critical speech aligns you with the accuser of the brethren. Prophetic ministry should never be a ministry of criticism, but rather of love.

## Are You Ready for More?

The depth and degree of your hunger for more of God is the length of your reach to Him. If you want to know more of God's revelatory ways, tell Him that you want your life to be a dwelling place for the Spirit, not just a guesthouse where He can show up every now and then. Tell Him that you want to become a permanent habitation of His prophetic grace.

He will come! He is jealous for His Bride and He is more than able to move obstacles of fear and unbelief and criticism and envy and competition in order to create a people for Himself, people who are secure in Him and always hungry for more, who are even eager to cheer each other on. Your growth and increase is my growth and increase, and mine is yours. We belong together, walking as closely with our Bridegroom as we can, so close that we can hear every whispered revelation.

## A Cry for Increase in God's Revelatory Ways

Father, I believe You want more of Your presence, Your giftings and Your revelatory ways to operate in my life. Toward that end, I align myself with Your grace, faith and purity, and I ask for a greater sensitivity to the voice of the Holy Spirit. I also ask for an increase of dreams and visions and visitations. I declare that increase is on the way, in Jesus' majestic name. Amen.

# 7

# Divine Insight

## *Praying in the Spirit*

*Y*ears ago after my wife and I had moved our young family to Kansas City, I had a dream in which the Holy Spirit spoke to me and said, "If you will pray two hours in the Spirit in one sitting, I will give you a spirit of revelation." Not realizing how difficult that would be, I was willing to give it a try. I felt I already had a spirit of revelation on my life, but I was quite eager for an increase of revelation from God.

Now, praying in the Spirit (praying in tongues) was not new to me, but praying for two hours straight was. I remember I had a stopwatch and I used it to clock the first fifteen minutes of prayer. *Whew!* I thought. *That fifteen minutes was hard, but it was good. I can do this.*

Later in the day, I would clock another fifteen minutes, and then another fifteen minutes, and another. To make two hours I had to pray eight of those fifteen-minute segments. At last by the end of the day, I had done my two hours. I went before

God and said something like this: "Hey, it's sort of like I did it. Yeah. So where's the increase?"

Then He reminded me of the word, which had said, "If you will pray two hours in the Spirit *in one sitting*, I will give you a spirit of revelation." Oh—in one sitting. That was going to take a little more work. I was going to have to build up my spiritual muscles in order to do that.

It was much harder than I anticipated. I could do the fifteen-minute segments all right, and then I worked my way up to half-hour segments. The big improvement came when I started singing in the Spirit as well. After adding the dimension of praise and worship to simply speaking my prayers in tongues, things shifted. It took repeated efforts, but eventually I could pray and sing in the Spirit for two hours solid. By then it was not a chore, but rather a delight.

As I practiced this new discipline, I began to have a dramatic increase of visions and revelation, including dreams in the night.

About that time, the Lord shifted gears on me again and He told me that whenever I was going to teach or preach publicly, He wanted me to pray in the Spirit for two hours beforehand. That entailed another shift of priorities. I was used to praying and reading the Bible by myself with no particular goal in mind, but now He was taking it into the public arena. He was showing me that any public ministry I had, far from being a performance, should express my lifestyle. He was showing me that my best ministry was reserved for Him; if I ministered to Him first, then I could do a much better job of ministering to others. I have kept this as a core value and it has steered my life ever since.

For that intense season, I really did do that. If I was preaching at 10:00 a.m. on a Sunday and I had to drive an hour to get there, I would get up by 6:00 a.m. so I could pray first. God was true to His word, because what I practiced in private produced fruit in public.

## Ninety Days of Solitary Confinement

Having grown my spiritual muscles somewhat and having learned a lot, a few years later I had another dream. In this dream, I was playing a game sort of like Monopoly. I saw a jail and a sign that said, "Do not pass Go. Do not collect $200." In this dream, the Holy Spirit told me that He was putting me in jail for ninety days and that I wouldn't be getting out.

At first I thought, *That doesn't sound like God. He doesn't put people in jail.* But when I found out what the jail sentence was, it sounded like God after all. He was not sentencing me to ninety days of solitary confinement because I had done something wrong. Instead, I was being taken into another "advanced class" of being in a cell alone with God.

He told me that being in solitary confinement meant that for the entire ninety days I would not be permitted to do public ministry. I would not be permitted to view or use any media, not even the phone. For the entire time, I was supposed to minister to the Lord.

Now, He did not tell me *how* to do it, so I had to figure that out. In the basement of our house I had a little office and I could lock the door from the inside. I arranged with Michal Ann that I would lock myself in there. We had three small children at that point, and I think she was pregnant with our fourth.

For those ninety days, I set myself to pray and sing in tongues for six to eighteen hours a day. I meditated on the Word and ministered to the Lord in any way I knew how to do.

Now, He has never asked me to do that since, but the fruit of that time was explosive. Divine information would run through my mind like ticker tape. The book of Leviticus came alive to me. Particular phrases, such as "fire on the altar" would come to my lips repeatedly, and later I preached messages and wrote books from all of the revelation that came during those three months.

117

## Scriptural Insights

The book of Jude has only one chapter, but it is full of revelation and divine insight about praying in the Spirit:

> But you, beloved, building yourselves up on your most holy faith, praying in the Holy Spirit, keep yourselves in the love of God, waiting anxiously for the mercy of our Lord Jesus Christ to eternal life.
>
> Jude 20–21

The wording catches my attention: "waiting anxiously." That does not contradict the Scriptures about casting your anxieties upon the Lord (see 1 Peter 5:7. See also Philippians 4:6; Matthew 6:25–34.) "Waiting anxiously" means waiting with expectation, hardly being able to contain your eagerness. Praying in the Spirit releases a supernatural atmosphere and enables you to walk continuously in the love of God.

Another interesting fact about this passage is that it says you are supposed to build yourself up. You cannot wait for others to do so, and you cannot wait for God to make it happen. Every one of us ebbs in our faith, but we can also grow in it. Even when we feel too low to figure out how to pray, we can pray in the Spirit.

The Spirit Himself will always help us:

> The Spirit also helps our weakness; for we do not know how to pray as we should, but the Spirit Himself intercedes for us with groanings too deep for words; and He who searches the hearts knows what the mind of the Spirit is, because He intercedes for the saints according to the will of God.
>
> Romans 8:26–27

It is true. We do not know how to pray as we should. We need fresh manna. We need to drop our agendas in favor of the

Lord's. If we want to know what is on His heart, one of the easiest ways to open the way is to pray in the Spirit.

Praying in the Spirit activates the grace of God to pray perfect prayers in any situation. These prayers go beyond our agendas and beyond our rational understanding. When we pray in the Spirit, divine insight enlightens our hearts so that we can hit the mark when we pray.

One of the Holy Spirit's primary responsibilities is to intercede continuously—for everything and everybody. I want to join Him and I hope you do, too.

I have learned a lot from these verses from Isaiah:

> Indeed, He will speak to this people through stammering lips and a foreign tongue, He who said to them, "Here is rest, give rest to the weary," and, "Here is repose," but they would not listen. So the word of the LORD to them will be, "Order on order, order on order, line on line, line on line, a little here, a little there," that they may go and stumble backward, be broken, snared and taken captive.
>
> Isaiah 28:11–13

Because it is so important, Paul picked up part of this passage and quoted it in his first letter to the Corinthian church. By the power of the Spirit, Paul the apostle takes the passage out of its historical context and brings it into play, first for the church at Corinth and then for the Church at large, which includes us in the 21st century. He wrote:

> In the Law it is written, "By men of strange tongues and by the lips of strangers I will speak to this people, and even so they will not listen to Me," says the Lord. So then tongues are for a sign, not to those who believe but to unbelievers.
>
> 1 Corinthians 14:21–22

When you pray in tongues, no longer will your mind be in overdrive. You will even sleep better. But the people around you may not understand what is going on.

119

The gift of tongues brings rest for the weary and refreshing peace. Indeed, "He will speak to this people through stammering lips and a foreign tongue" (Isaiah 28:11–12). And his unsurpassed peace quiets our spirits, which creates a perfect incubation environment for more revelation.

We take coffee breaks. Why not take prayer breaks? The people around us will benefit, and so will we. Let's seek divine insight purposefully by praying in the Spirit.

## Defining the Gift of Tongues

We need to make sure we are talking about the same thing when we talk about praying in the Spirit.

"Praying in the Spirit" is the same as praying in tongues. Some of the New Testament references to the gift of tongues refer to public utterances, while others refer only to the private, devotional use of the gift. (This does not imply that two different gifts are involved, however. Any person who speaks publicly in tongues also uses the gift in private.[1]) Besides using the gift in private devotions, we also pray Spirit-inspired intercessory prayers by using the gift of tongues.

The gift of tongues is a gift for everybody. Just as every believer is meant to be filled with the Holy Spirit, so every believer has the option of speaking in tongues. Some argue that the gift is the only true proof of being baptized in the Spirit. I will not go that far, but I will say that it is a very good evidence of someone having been baptized in the Spirit.

The gift is miraculous, definitely. Ordinary people, regardless of their educational background, can speak in tongues; some of them may not have even learned to read and write. Without opening a language book or living in a foreign country, the Holy Spirit enables them to begin to speak in another language—and they can continue to speak in this language whenever they want to. They can't understand what they're speaking, but they can speak expressively and smoothly. Their particular tongue may be identifiable as a known language, and on occasion they may be understood by a native speaker. Or it may be a heavenly language, one of the "tongues of angels" (see 1 Corinthians 13:1). Almost never is a person's God-given tongue a language that that person has learned to speak, even in part. Speaking in tongues has nothing whatsoever to do with linguistic ability.[2]

John Wimber, founder of the Vineyard churches, called it "kinds of tongues" to emphasize the plurality of the expression of tongues. "Kinds of tongues," he taught, "are Spirit-inspired, spontaneous utterances in which the conscious mind plays no part. It is speaking in a language (whether earthly or angelic) which the speaker has never learned or understood. This is used privately by the believer and may be used at will for his own edification. Tongues are also used in public as an ecstatic utterance following an anointing from God."

In his book, *The Holy Spirit Today,* Dick Iverson defined the gift of tongues like this:

> The gift of tongues is the God-given enablement to communicate in a language one does not know. . . . This is a "manifestation of the Spirit" (1 Corinthians 12:7) and not human ability. It has absolutely nothing to do with natural linguistic ability, eloquence of speech or a new sanctified way of talking. . . . The gift of tongues is a supernatural manifestation or expression of the Holy Spirit through a person's speech organs.[3]

### The Purpose of Praying in the Spirit

Have you ever wondered how you can obey scriptural exhortations to "pray at all times"? "With all prayer and petition," writes Paul in the book of Ephesians, "pray at all times in the Spirit, and with this in view, be on the alert with all perseverance and petition for all the saints" (Ephesians 6:18). The only way I know how to do it is to pray in tongues wherever you go. Whether out loud or silently, you can keep up a steady stream of prayer when you let the Spirit flow through you. Unlike you and me, He is not distractible.

You can be changing your baby's diapers and praying in tongues, driving your car and praying in tongues, balancing your checkbook and praying in tongues. Praying in the Spirit heightens your alertness, which in turn helps you do everything from mundane tasks to moving mountains by faith. It is important to persevere, even if you are not called to pray in the Spirit in an intensive way as I was for that season in my life.

The fact is, your prayer life will fall flat unless you have the Holy Spirit helping you. The Spirit fills you so that He can be the Lord of your praying. Andrew Murray wrote, "The connection between the prayer life and the spirit life is close and indissolvable."[4] Christ Jesus becomes your very life (see Romans 8:2; Colossians 3:4), and the Spirit makes you spiritually healthy.

The Holy Spirit draws you to prayer, ever wooing and enticing you to come to Him, and He is the one who ushers you into the presence of the Father. Without Him we could not enter freely into the presence of the glory. It is not too much to say that the Holy Spirit gives you special access to the Lord:

> And He came and preached peace to you who were far away, and peace to those who were near; for through Him we both have our access in one Spirit to the Father . . . in whom we have boldness and confident access through faith in Him.
>
> Ephesians 2:17–18; 3:12

The Spirit teaches you to pray by causing you to breathe in the atmosphere of the Spirit and breathe out the spirit of prayer. We call the Spirit the *parakletos* or *paraclete*, the Counselor and Teacher (see John 14:26), because He helps you in your petitions. How much help will He provide? As Charles Finney wrote, "He will give you as much of the spirit of prayer as you have strength of body to bear."[5]

When the Holy Spirit burdens you to pray, your heart begins to beat with His. The Spirit longs to share His burdens, His compassion and His travail with you so that you can identify with the brokenness of the world and carry God's compassionate heart to it.

**Ways to Pray in the Spirit**

We have already looked at praying in the Spirit for personal devotional communion, which is depicted in the following Scriptures:

- Isaiah 28:11–13 (Praying in the Spirit releases rest and refreshment.)
- Jude 20 (Praying in the Spirit builds up our faith and love while granting us revelation of the mercy of God.)
- 1 Corinthians 14:1–4 (Praying in the Spirit enables us to speak mysteries to God and, at the same time, it edifies us.)
- 1 Corinthians 14:15 (When you are praying in tongues, your spirit is praying.)

Then there is praying in the Spirit for the sake of intercessory prayer. I break this down into three kinds of intercession: revelatory (God-inspired) prayer, compassionate intercession and spiritual breakthrough prayer.

The first one, revelatory prayer, can be known as prophetic intercession. This is when you feel urged by the Spirit to pray for a situation about which you have very little actual knowledge; you are praying for the prayer requests that are on the heart of

God. Why does He nudge you to pray? So that He can intervene. In this way any of us can pray to help bring forth His will on the earth as it is willed in heaven.

When your heart is stirred by a circumstance to weeping, brokenness and tearful groaning, often that means that you are sensing the Lord's heart in the situation. With deep emotion, you cry out for the Lord's intervention into that state of affairs.

On occasion, a spiritual warfare anointing may come upon you. Praying in tongues may be coupled with a gift of faith and a gift of discerning of spirits. Your travailing prayer opens the way for the purposes of God to come forth. Demonic powers flee. Activated in times of individual deliverance or strategic spiritual warfare, this form of praying in the Spirit addresses the powers of darkness over individuals, families, cities and people groups.

In addition to these specific ways of praying in the Spirit, I must not forget to mention *exalting* God in tongues. When Peter preached to Cornelius' household, he and his companions were stunned when the Gentiles were filled with the Spirit, "for they were hearing them speaking with tongues and exalting God" (Acts 10:46). Praying in the Spirit enables us to say "I love You" to God in a way that is not limited by the language or languages we have learned, such as English. In any human language, you can say "I love You; I adore You; I give myself to You" in only a limited way. But praying in tongues takes the limits off—it is a great thing to do!

On occasion, especially in a public setting, an expression in tongues will be interpreted into English (or whatever language understood by the hearers) by someone who exercises the gift of interpretation of tongues. This bumps prayer in the Spirit into the realm of prophecy:

> Now I wish that you all spoke in tongues, but even more that you
> would prophesy; and greater is one who prophesies than one

who speaks in tongues, unless he interprets, so that the church may receive edifying. . . . So also you, since you are zealous of spiritual gifts, seek to abound for the edification of the church.

1 Corinthians 14:5, 12

Kenneth Hagin used to explain it this way, "Two nickels equal one dime. However, the two nickels are not a ten-cent piece. Prophecy is the dime, the ten-cent piece. Naturally, it would be better to have the dime (prophecy) than to have the nickel (an utterance in tongues). But, if interpretation (another nickel) went along with it, then the two would be equivalent to the dime."[6]

## The Power of Inspired Prayer

In my experience (and that of many others) praying in tongues can result in powerful, specific revelation that aids and inspires prayerful intervention in a crisis situation.

My best personal example of this happened in 1987 during the war between Iraq and Iran in the Persian Gulf. At the time, I did not know the names of the countries in that region, nor did I understand the seriousness of the situation there. I was with some fellow intercessors at the Ukrainian Pentecostal Church in Manhattan, and we were praying in tongues. In fact, I was on the floor for about five hours, praying in tongues quietly.

While I was praying in the Spirit, I kept seeing in my mind's eye a picture of a map of the Middle East. I could not see it clearly, so I was trying to get a better view of it, not to mention an understanding of what to do with what I was seeing.

"Knowings" kept coming to me. I became convinced that I was glimpsing a critical circumstance. As I kept peering at the map in my mind's eye, I noticed something that looked like a tiny island nation. I could see letters spelling out B-a-h-r-a-i, and then a final letter. I could not tell if it was an "n" or an "m."

I sensed in the Spirit that there was a U.S. military presence in this tiny nation, which was unknown to me.

I knew that Iran was being pressured by the prince of Persia, the demonic principality mentioned in the book of Daniel (see Daniel 10:13), to initiate an unprovoked attack against the United States in this tiny island nation that could catapult us prematurely into World War III before God's appointed time. That is a pretty heavy thing to be picking up on, and the revelation would not cease; it kept coming to me.

After five hours, I told my friends what I was seeing. They did not know about this island nation, either, nor did they know much about what was going on there. But they believed it was from God, and they laid their hands on me so that I could pray into this situation. This was a special situation, seeing as how it fell far outside of my normal sphere of authority. And the Holy Spirit clothed me with supernatural power, putting into my hands (in the Spirit) a bow and arrow. Clothed with the armor of God, I pulled back the bowstring and said, "I shoot the arrow into the prince of Persia and I command you to back off the tiny island nation of Bahrai-something." I felt a release of power go out from me; we all felt it. Then that mantle of authority lifted off me and I wondered what had just happened.

We were hungry after praying since early in the morning, so we started across the street to get something to eat. Along the way there was a newspaper stand and on it was a peach-colored newspaper called the *Financial Times* of London, England. I bought one, and I have it to this day. On the front page, the headline read, "Tehran Threatens to Retaliate against U.S. for Ship Attack." In the middle of the page the subheadline stated, "American Navy in Second Confrontation." Then it showed a map of the Middle East and spoke of the U.S. Naval Command in a place called Bahrain, an archipelago of islands in the Persian Gulf.

Although no American newspaper that I ever saw carried this report, the lead story of the *Financial Times*, dated September 23, 1987, read:

> In a lengthy address to the U.N. General Assembly on the seventh anniversary of the start of the Gulf war, [Iranian head of state] Khomeini repeatedly denounced the U.N. and the U.N. Security Council in the bitterest of terms. Departing from his prepared text he said, "I want to draw urgent attention to the very grave and immediate danger provoked by the U.S. Administration's latest action which is very dangerous to the whole world. . . . This is a beginning for a series of events, the bitter consequences of which shall not be confined to the Persian Gulf, and the U.S. as the initiator shall bear responsibility for all ensuing events. I declare here that the U.S. shall receive a proper response for this evil act.[7]

That planned attack did not happen. Not only that, but quite likely because of other people around the world praying, the tension in that region de-escalated and an international war was averted. That revelation was 100 percent accurate, and I have kept that newspaper to this day.

I have had other experiences like this over the years, and so have other people. Crisis intervention through Spirit-led prayer is real and effective.

## Let the Hand of God Come upon You

In Hebrew, there is a word for "hand" that refers to the burden of the Lord: *massa*. This word refers specifically to the way the Lord's presence comes upon you and imparts something so that even when His hand lifts, the burden remains. That is how prophetic intercession works—divine insight comes to inform powerful prayers.

Here is what James the apostle wrote about it in his epistle:

127

The effective prayer of a righteous man can accomplish much. Elijah was a man with a nature like ours, and he prayed earnestly that it would not rain, and it did not rain on the earth for three years and six months. Then he prayed again, and the sky poured rain and the earth produced its fruit.

James 5:16–18

Never put limits on what God can do, even through an ordinary person like you!

## A Prayer for Divine Insight

Heavenly Father, in the name of the Lord Jesus Christ, I ask for an increase of divine insight as I pray in the Spirit. Let Your hand come upon me and let the burden of the Lord be deposited with me. I ask for greater clarity, revelation and discernment to pray fervent, effective prayers. Thank You, Lord. Amen and Amen!

# 8

# Israel

## *God's Prophetic Calendar*

*E*arly in my ministry, I sat under some of the best teachers on the topic of Israel, the Middle East and the relevant scriptural prophecies, but I never felt I needed to address the subject myself. *Why should I?* I thought, since I was surrounded by such experts.

We hosted invitation-only prayer retreats in those days, where we would come together for teaching, worship and fellowship. Often we would simply come before God to seek His face, with no agenda in mind.

One of these retreats was held in the Atlanta, Georgia area. We called it A Cry to the Lord. I was scheduled to speak in the evening session. During the time of worship, led by Avner and Rachel Boskey of Beer-Sheva, Israel, I saw a vision of an angel standing in the corner of the room during worship. This angel was dressed in a brilliant white wedding garment, and I heard these words in my heart: "I have come to release a message on the wedding of the Church and Israel." That evening, I delivered my first message on "The Mystery of the Church and Israel" and my heart was enlarged with God's love.

I am not one of those romanticists regarding Israel, someone who views the Jewish people through rose-colored lenses and who does not think Israel can do anything wrong. But I do not want to neglect to love Israel (or the Palestinians, either). God's heart of love holds the whole world, and I believe He wants all of us to grow in our love for the nations.

When you love, you give, and that is what God did when He gave His only begotten Son. When we love Israel and the peoples of the Middle East, one of the ways we can give is to intercede in prayer for them.

No set of teachings combining the themes of intercession and the prophetic would be complete without considering the biblical centerpiece of Israel. Israel is not optional. The story of the nation of Israel is the story of the culmination of God's purposes for the entire earth.

## A Brief Overview

The board has been set and the pieces are moving. Throughout the ages, it seems as if God has been waiting for His strategic moment. He is positioning His intercessory knights and prophetic bishops together for a sweeping move—one that all the world will observe closely. No eye will miss the mysterious and fascinating day on God's prophetic calendar when He once again steps into the world of space and time. It is time for the unveiling of the mystery of Israel as the apple of God's eye (see Zechariah 2:8), the crucial piece on God's chessboard.

Although modern Israel was only seventy years old as of 2018, the Jewish nation is actually one of the oldest on earth. These people and their land reach back to the time of

Abraham's epic pilgrimage and the covenant promise of God to him and his descendants (see Genesis 17:4–8). After what many considered to be a silence of two thousand years, this land has been reborn. Israel is once again on display before the eyes of the world.

How could a remnant of scattered and persecuted Jewish people, who went through their darkest hour in Hitler's Holocaust, suddenly regain their sovereign nation within their ancient territory? Not without divine intervention, for sure, although many Israelis today believe they did it all on their own. Let's take a brief look at the modern history of this region.

On November 29, 1947, the General Assembly of the United Nations adopted a resolution requiring the establishment of a Jewish state in Palestine. The following is a portion of the Proclamation of Independence read by David Ben-Gurion on May 14, 1948:

> The land of Israel was the birthplace of the Jewish people. Here their spiritual, religious and national identity was formed. Here they achieved independence and created a culture of national and universal significance. Here they wrote and gave the Bible to the world. Exiled from the Land of Israel, the Jewish people remained faithful to it in all the countries of their dispersion, never ceasing to pray and hope for their return and the restoration of their national freedom.
>
> Our call goes out to the Jewish people all over the world to rally to our side in the task of immigration and development and to stand by us in the great struggle for the fulfillment of the dream of generations for the redemption of Israel. With trust in Almighty God, we set our hand to this Declaration on the Sabbath eve, the fifth of Iyar, 5708, the fourteenth day of May, 1948.[1]

Just a day later, on May 15, 1948, five Arab nations assaulted the newborn state. Egypt, Syria, Jordan, Lebanon and Iraq

(40 million Arabs, 1.5 million of them armed) attacked Israel in what became known as the Israeli War of Independence. The war continued for eight months with heavy casualties on all sides. The miracle is that Israel, which had just been reborn, could not be destroyed (see Isaiah 54:17).

### A Look behind the Scenes

I wonder what was going on behind the scenes in prayer as the United Nations made this historic decision. Let's part the veil and peer into some prayer history. A Welshman named Rees Howells gave his life to the Lord Jesus and dedicated it to intercession. Few in modern history have changed lives and affected nations with the authority of prayer like this believer. Let us look at this historic time through his eyes.

> After the war was over in October and November in 1947, whole days were given to prayer. On eleven different days during those two months, prayer was concentrated on the coming U. N. vote. When on November 27th the news came through that the partition of Palestine had not been carried, the whole Bible College, of which Rees Howells was the founder and principal, gave themselves to intense intercession. In prayer they actually became aware of God's angels influencing the men in the U. N. debate. Before hearing the final outcome they already had full assurance of victory. When on November 29th the news came that the partition proposal had been carried, the College claimed it as one of the greatest days for God in 1900 years![2]

Amazing, isn't it? Prophetic intercessors carry God's heart for Israel!

### Disaster Averted

In 1967 the Six-Day War should also have ended in disaster for Israel, but again God's mercy prevailed. Israel not only defeated her enemies, but captured Sinai, the Gaza Strip, the West Bank and the Golan Heights in only six days. They also captured the Jewish quarter of Jerusalem and the remaining Western (Wailing) Wall of the Temple. At this point, the Israelis controlled all holy Jewish and Christian sites.

And consider the outcome of the surprise 1973 Yom Kippur assault. A coalition of Arab nations led by Egypt and Syria and backed by one of the world's two nuclear superpowers, the Soviet Union, attacked on two fronts; but Israel again came back from the brink of defeat to emerge victorious. Attacking Israel by surprise on her holiest day, the Arabs forced the Israelis back and made brief territorial gains. Yet by what I believe was divine intervention, Israel regained all her land. Once again the hand of God, working in part through human beings, protected the outnumbered and despised Jewish nation.

Still to this day, the enemies of Israel are stirred up. In the words of the psalm:

> They make shrewd plans against Your people, and conspire together against Your treasured ones. They have said, "Come, and let us wipe them out as a nation, that the name of Israel be remembered no more."

> Psalm 83:3–4

Sometimes they use those very words, whether or not they realize they are using the words of a psalm. Jihadists and Islamic terrorists continue to declare their goal, to wipe Israel off the face of the earth.

## Prophetic Foresight

God's promise to once again gather and protect the nation of Israel is a declaration of His faithfulness and greatness, not Israel's perfection. With this in mind, let's look at some significant Old Testament prophecies regarding Israel's dispersion and regathering.

Jeremiah, the weeping prophet, glimpsed the future and saw that Israel's faithful, covenant-keeping God would once again offer divine protection to His people in the Promised Land:

> Hear the word of the LORD, O nations, and declare in the coastlands afar off, and say, "He who scattered Israel will gather him and keep him as a shepherd keeps his flock."
>
> Jeremiah 31:10

We find three truths contained in this one verse from Jeremiah. First, it was God Himself who scattered Israel from her own homeland. Second, the same God who scattered Israel will regather her to her own land. And third, God will put a divine hedge of protection around her during the process.

## Two Regatherings Predicted

With the theme of God's grace and His faithfulness in mind, let's back up and look at the Diaspora (the dispersion) of the Jewish people in history.

### The First Regathering

It is my understanding that Scripture tells us the Jews would suffer two major dispersions, or scatterings, followed by two regatherings.

The first scattering occurred in the years when the prophets Daniel and Ezekiel were exiled in the land of Babylon. This was also the period in which the Jews of the Judean kingdom were displaced from their country after Nebuchadnezzar destroyed the Temple, Jerusalem and the commonwealth (see Daniel 1:1–6). Daniel and his associates were kidnapped around 605 BC.

The Jews began to return to the land in 538 BC (see 2 Chronicles 36:22–23; Ezra 1:1–4), and the Temple remained flattened until 515 BC (see Ezra 6:15), about seventy years after its destruction.

The prophet Daniel was held captive in Babylon—a foreign land with foreign gods and culture. After decades of captivity, while meditating on the Word of God (see Daniel 9:2), Daniel received a revelation from the prophetic promises of Jeremiah:

> "This whole land will be a desolation and a horror, and these nations will serve the king of Babylon seventy years. Then it will be when seventy years are completed I will punish the king of Babylon and that nation," declares the LORD.
>
> Jeremiah 25:11–12

> Thus says the LORD, "When seventy years have been completed for Babylon, I will visit you and fulfill My good word to you, to bring you back to this place."
>
> Jeremiah 29:10

Daniel believed the Word and declared it as revealed to Jeremiah—that at the end of seventy years of Babylonian captivity, the children of Israel would be released to return to their own land. Daniel also sought the Lord to reveal any obstacles to the prophetic promise being fulfilled (see Daniel 9:3–19). Daniel then responded to the prophetic word by confessing the sin of his people as his own. The verse that summarizes his confession is Daniel 9:19, which reads as follows:

> O Lord, hear! O Lord, forgive! O Lord, listen and take action! For Your own sake, O my God, do not delay, because Your city and Your people are called by Your name.

The fact that Jeremiah spoke accurately and Daniel later prayed based on those words is an example of prophetic intercession at its best. God did precisely what His prophets said

He would do. At the end of seventy years the Israelites fulfilled the prophecy of their first return to their covenant land. They began to rebuild the walls of Jerusalem.

Israel continued in many more years of faith, sin, repentance, revival and restoration, but the word of the Lord had been fulfilled and God had shown Himself true to His promise.

### The Second Regathering

That was not the only dispersion and regathering prophesied by God's watchmen. Isaiah states that the Lord would set His hand a second time to recover a remnant of His people:

> It will happen on that day that the Lord will again recover the second time with His hand the remnant of His people, who will remain, from Assyria, Egypt, Pathros, Cush, Elam, Shinar, Hamath, and from the islands of the sea. And He will lift up a standard for the nations and assemble the banished ones of Israel, and will gather the dispersed of Judah *from the four corners of the earth.*
>
> Isaiah 11:11–12, emphasis added

This Scripture clearly describes a second dispersion and, at some point, a second regathering. The first dispersion did not send these Jews in many directions at once. They remained together—a persecuted yet identifiable people in a foreign nation. But the second scattering would send them to regions beyond the known world of Isaiah's day—to the four corners of the earth. It is my understanding (as well as that of many others) that we are seeing this second great regathering being fulfilled in this generation.

Let's make it simple. The Scriptures explain that there would be a regional dispersion followed by a regional regathering. Then there would be a worldwide dispersion followed by a worldwide regathering. When did the second dispersion occur? It began around AD 70 under the Roman general Titus, when the Jewish people once again fled their homeland and ran for their lives. For approximately nineteen hundred years, they had no political autonomy and were scattered to the four corners of the earth.

Ramon Bennett wrote of this second gathering in his book *When Day and Night Cease*:

> The second gathering began with the trickle of Jews into Palestine after the turn of the last century. The trickle became a stream after 1948 and then a river during the 1950s and 1960s. The river is now in flood stage and in danger of bursting its banks with the masses arriving from the last vestiges of the (former) Soviet Union.[3]

I love it when the purposes of God unfold right in front of our eyes! That is exactly what I see occurring in the Middle East today.

## A Divine Appointment

Let me pause for a moment and tell you about something that took place when I returned from my first trip to Israel in 1987. Though this was years ago, I hope you will pick up a little more of God's heart for Israel as I relay this fascinating encounter.

On my return flight from that first trip to Israel, I was mistakenly bumped up to first class. What an accidental blessing—and a divine appointment! I ended up sitting next to a distinguished gentleman, and my spiritual antennas began buzzing. I knew nothing about him but felt a curious desire to share from the prophetic Scriptures.

"Would you like to know what's next on God's prophetic calendar?" I asked.

He looked at me intently with curiosity. So I began to tell him that Russia and the Eastern European countries would be freed from the grip of Communism and that an exodus of the Jewish people of grand proportions would soon be occurring from the biblical "land of the north." Quoting from Isaiah and Jeremiah, I told him that circumstances in the Middle East would change radically as a result.

Since my neighbor appeared to be listening intently, I continued talking. What would jump out of my mouth next?

### Fishermen and Hunters

I took him to Jeremiah 16:14–16, which states:

"Therefore behold, days are coming," declares the LORD, "when it will no longer be said, 'As the LORD lives, who brought up the sons of Israel out of the land of Egypt,' but, 'As the LORD lives, who brought up the sons of Israel from the land of the north and from all the countries where He had banished them.' For I will restore them to their own land which I gave to their fathers. Behold, I am going to send for many fishermen," declares the LORD, "and they will fish for them; and afterwards I will send for many hunters, and they will hunt them from every mountain and every hill and from the clefts of the rocks."

Rarely have I had such an attentive audience. The fellow leaned toward me as if to say, "Is there more?" I plowed ahead, explaining my understanding of these verses, as the Holy Spirit seemed to rest quietly on me.

I began to talk about the terms *fishermen* and *hunters* as stated in Jeremiah, and what they could possibly mean. I told him that the fishermen in Jeremiah were sent out to call the Jewish people to return to their homeland. In fact, one of the first "fishermen" spoke as early as 1897 when secular leader Theodor Herzl released an early call at the first World Zionist Congress held in Basil, Switzerland, for the establishment of a Jewish state. The next major move on the divine chessboard happened in 1917 when General Allenby and the British forces liberated Jerusalem from four hundred years of Turkish domination. They signed the Balfour Declaration calling for a national home for the Jews.

I went on to explain that in 1933 Zeb Jabotinsky, one of the early Jewish pioneers in Palestine, warned the Jews of Germany: "There is no future for you here. Come back to your land while the doors are still open."[4]

The times changed at that point, from the fishermen of mercy to the hunters of judgment. What followed eventually led to the slaughter of six million Jews.

### God's Great Treasure

After hearing about the fishermen and hunters, the gentleman seated next to me pulled out his notebook, took a few notes. Then he closed his pad and began to probe gently, asking who I was, what I was doing on this trip and whether I had talked with any international military leaders.

I realized I had struck a nerve, but had no idea that this was a man of tremendous influence and responsibility. In fact, this man turned out to be the deputy secretary of the Joint Chiefs of Staff in President Reagan's administration, in charge of military strategy in the Middle East.

I must admit, it was kind of exciting! I believe the Lord wanted him to know what was coming next. As I shared from the Scriptures with him, I knew some of God's great treasure was being placed into his heart.

In addition, my own appetite was whetted for more divine appointments. May He lead each of us into opportunities to draw people's attention to Israel!

### More about the Second Regathering

Back to our main topic: what the prophetic Scriptures say about the second regathering. Jeremiah's trumpet sends out a clarion call:

"Behold, I am bringing them from the north country, and I will gather them from the remote parts of the earth, among them the blind and the lame, the woman with child and she who is in labor with child, together; a great company, they will return here. With weeping they will come, and by supplication I will lead them; I will make them walk by streams of waters, on a straight path in which they will not stumble; for I am a father to Israel, and Ephraim is My firstborn."

Hear the word of the LORD, O nations, and declare in the coastlands afar off, and say, "He who scattered Israel will gather him and keep him as a shepherd keeps his flock."

Jeremiah 31:8–10

These verses specifically mention "the north country" as one of the primary places of exodus and returning. To understand the regions involved, we must look at the map. It is interesting to note that Moscow is located directly north of Israel.

Jeremiah explained more about how God's people would be led out: "With weeping they will come, and by supplication I will lead them" (verse 9). What is supplication? *Strong's Concordance* renders the meaning of this word simply as "strong prayer." Awesome! Once again we are given the secret of the fulfillment of the prophetic promise: the desperate prayer of the heart (weeping) and praying the promise back to God (supplication). Here again we find God's purposes birthed through prophetic intercession. History continues to unfold as intercessors pave the way for prophetic fulfillment.

## Prophetic Promises for the Hope of Israel

God is calling us to participate in making history. A whole lot more of God's prophetic word is going to be fulfilled, but He is waiting to hear His intercessors remind Him of the appointments on His calendar (the Bible) that have not yet been

140

accomplished. As prophetic intercessors and as watchmen on the walls, we are called to remind the Lord of His promises and appointments. That means we need to get to know the Word of God—and the God of the Word.

We can pray straight from Scripture. For example, we can pray these words about the regathering from Isaiah:

> Do not fear, for I am with you; I will bring your offspring from the east, and gather you from the west. I will say to the north, "Give them up!" And to the south, "Do not hold them back." Bring My sons from afar and My daughters from the ends of the earth.
>
> Isaiah 43:5–6

Or from Jeremiah:

> "Therefore behold, the days are coming," declares the Lord, "when they will no longer say, 'As the Lord lives, who brought up the sons of Israel from the land of Egypt,' but, 'As the Lord lives, who brought up and led back the descendants of the household of Israel from the north land and from all the countries where I had driven them.' Then they will live on their own soil."
>
> Jeremiah 23:7–8

The prophetic Word tells us that when the people of Israel are once again living on their own soil, we will see a global outpouring of the Holy Spirit. Israel is God's timepiece, and in terms of salvation, the world moves according to God's prophetic calendar, which is linked to the times of the Gentiles being fulfilled (see Romans 11). In a time of crisis, blinders will come off eyes and not only the Jewish people but also the Arabs will lift a cry to the Lord. And as Paul told us, "whosoever shall call upon the name of the Lord shall be saved" (Romans 10:13 KJV).

Paul the apostle admonished the Roman church (and all believers) to pray with God's heart, writing, "Brethren, my heart's desire and prayer to God for Israel is that they may be saved" (Romans 10:1 NKJV).

The words of the prophet Zechariah will be fulfilled:

> I will pour out on the house of David and on the inhabitants of Jerusalem, the Spirit of grace and of supplication, so that they will look on Me whom they have pierced; and they will mourn for Him, as one mourns for an only son, and they will weep bitterly over Him like the bitter weeping over a firstborn.
>
> Zechariah 12:10

Salvation comes only through our Messiah, Jesus Christ. We can say with Paul therefore: "I am not ashamed of the gospel, for it is the power of God for salvation to everyone who believes, to the Jew first and also to the Greek" (Romans 1:16).

## Proclaim, Praise and Pray

Always remember that little keys open big doors. Then look for the keys you need to unlock the promises of God. Jeremiah 31:7 perhaps summarizes better than any other verse the believer's practical response to God's prophetic invitation:

> Thus says the LORD, "Sing aloud with gladness for Jacob, and shout among the chief of the nations; proclaim, give praise and say, 'O LORD, save Your people, the remnant of Israel.'"

This verse points out three important and distinct actions. They are the words *proclaim*, *praise* and *say*. The word *say* in this context refers to prayer, since we are exhorted through "saying" to talk to God. God gives us three successive keys to insert into the prison door on behalf of the Jewish people, to help deliver them into God's destiny. These keys are *the power of proclamation, the power of praise* and *the power of prayer.*

Like Elijah, call for the drought to end and for a time of mercy to begin. Pray for the peace of Jerusalem. Let the Holy Spirit tune your heart to heaven. May *Elohim*, the Creator and Supreme Being, give you the spirit of wisdom and revelation concerning His prophetic calendar for Israel, and may His heart for Jerusalem beat in your own as you help give birth to God's purposes through prophetic intercession.

**A Prayer for the Jewish People**

Father, in the name of Jesus the Messiah, I ask You to bring me into alignment with Your Word concerning Your heart for Israel and the Jewish people. I thank You that I live in a time when the prophetic Scriptures are being fulfilled right before our very eyes! I want to be properly tuned in to Your prophetic purposes for this generation. I pray that, for the rest of our days, we will never return to old ways of anti-Semitism in the Church, but rather that those of us who are Gentiles will carry the Jewish people upon our shoulders. I receive this burden of the Lord with grace and thanksgiving. Amen.

*Part 3*

# A Heart for
# Prophetic Intercession

*I*n the first eight chapters of this book, we have been exploring what it means to have God's heart for intercession (Part 1) and God's heart for the prophetic (Part 2). Now it is time to put them together.

In Part 3 we will wrap up our discoveries by considering what it means to have a heart for prophetic intercession. We will culminate our journey of discovery with a whole chapter devoted to having "A Heart for His Presence," in which we will learn how to cultivate hearts that want nothing more than to be doorkeepers in the house of God. After all, "better is one day in your courts than a thousand elsewhere; I would rather be a doorkeeper in the house of my God than dwell in the tents of the wicked" (Psalm 84:10 NIV).

Our hearts are meant to do this—to be faithful doorkeepers of the presence of God not only for our personal lives but also for the lives of our family members and fellow citizens. As prophetic intercessors, we bear the heart of God for the whole world, and we contribute in an ongoing way to answering Jesus' request in His model prayer, known to us as the Lord's Prayer. To sum up, we are helping to "pray in" the Kingdom of God: "Thy kingdom come. Thy will be done in earth, as it is in heaven" (Matthew 6:10 KJV).

Friends, as disciples of the Lord Jesus Christ, each of us is called to be a watchman on the walls as a prophetic intercessor. Let's lean into the heart of Jesus so that we can release prayers that "strike the mark," causing His will to be done on earth as it is in heaven.

With this in mind, join me now in praying prayers of prophetic intercession, calling for the Kingdom of heaven to come on earth!

# 9

# The Power of
# Prophetic Intercession

One of the most significant yet little-known characters in the New Testament is the prophetess Anna. After seven years of married life, she was suddenly widowed. We do not know how she lost her husband, if she had children or whether she was left all alone. All we are told is that this unassuming 84-year-old woman had devoted the rest of her years to the ministry of prayer and fasting, waiting in the Temple for the coming of the Messiah.

> There was a prophetess, Anna the daughter of Phanuel, of the tribe of Asher. She was advanced in years and had lived with her husband seven years after her marriage, and then as a widow to the age of eighty-four. She never left the temple, serving night and day with fastings and prayers.
>
> Luke 2:36–37

We do not know the age at which Anna got married. In all likelihood she was young, possibly seventeen or even younger. If so, she was widowed at least by the age of 24 and then devoted the next sixty years of her life to priestly intercession. In the event that she married a little later in life, let's say at 37, she would still have been widowed at 44 and have spent forty years waiting in the Temple.

Whew! Whether it was forty years or sixty, she had been at the Temple for a long time, crying out to the Lord day and night with prayer and fasting. What kind of a burning passion must have consumed Anna's heart to keep her there for such a long time? Then after years of what some would call futile idleness, her waiting paid off.

It takes a prophetic vision to continue such a ministry long-term. You must have a clear revelation regarding your target, purpose and goal. Burdens and crises are not enough; they come and go. What motivates intercessors over the long haul? Only one thing. Like the praying prophetess Anna we must have a consuming vision of the One we serve. First and foremost we need a vision of our Lord Himself. After all, He is the goal and prize of life. With our eyes fixed on Him, we will be ready for His summons.

In what way can Anna be considered a prophetess? The Scripture does not tell us that she wore a coat of camel's hair or ate locusts and wild honey. I doubt that she pointed a gnarled finger at people, declaring, "Thus saith the Lord!" and revealing the secret sins of their hearts. We have no written evidence that she ever confronted the prophets of Baal like Elijah of old or called down fire from heaven. In fact, we find not even one word of recorded prophecy from this devout woman.

If she did not give personal prophetic words, then what was her prophetic ministry? She was a woman of the secret place, not one with a public ministry at all, one who interceded with the purposes of God for her generation. The expression of her prophetic ministry was her enduring intercession. She was a prophetic, intercessory Jesus fanatic!

Here is what happened when Joseph and Mary brought eight-day-old Jesus to the Temple to present Him to the Lord:

> At that very moment [Anna] came up and began giving thanks to God, and continued to speak of Him to all those who were looking for the redemption of Jerusalem.
>
> Luke 2:38

Undoubtedly Anna's intercessory burden had included searching through the prophetic promises that had not yet been fulfilled. This verse in Luke tells us that she "continued to speak of [Jesus] to all those who were looking for the redemption of Jerusalem." You see, Anna was looking for a Deliverer, the Messiah, the hope of Israel. She was one of a special task force of prophetic intercessors whom God had ordained for that generation. They were the ones who were listening and watching for the Lord's appearing. Like Joshua they were waiting at the doorway of the tent of meeting in hopes that they would be the first to see the Lord's great presence. Anna was doubtless praying through those beloved prophetic promises of a coming Messiah.

The Lord is searching for an "Anna Company" in our day, intercessors who will pray through the promises of the Second Coming of our long-expected Lord and Messiah. Who will pave the way for the coming of the Lord? New recruits are wanted and the Holy Spirit is sending out invitations today.

Many of the greatest intercessors of our time have been women. Their sensitivity of spirit, their passion for the things of God, the readiness with which they yield their hearts to Him to plead His cause—all these characteristics serve intercessors well. It was a woman who anointed Christ for burial. Women remained at the cross when the rest of the disciples fled. Women were the first to proclaim, "He is risen!"

The real issue, of course, is not whether you are male or female. To be part of this "Anna Company," all you need is an ever-growing conviction of the purposes of God and a desire to pray through God's promises until you see them fulfilled. In our day and time the Holy Spirit is drawing together a people who will stand united in a congregation, city or region. God is wooing believers to one another as covenant prayer partners. He is summoning the leaders in an area to stand together and fight. He is calling all of us in His Body to join hands and take our places until the promises of a great, end-time visitation for our generation have come to pass.

### Priest, Prophet, Intercessor

Let's summarize a few thoughts on how the tasks of priests and prophets in the Old Testament can help us understand our assignment to be intercessors, specifically prophetic intercessors. I touched on this back in the fifth chapter.

The job of the *priest* is to plead the needs of the people before the Lord. He does not represent himself, but rather he carries the burdens, needs and cares of others before our majestic God. As priests, our hearts pulse with the needs of our cities, congregations and nations. As New Testament priests, we represent others to God.

What is the job of the *prophet*? He represents the interests of God to the people. Having stood in the council of the Almighty, the prophet releases what is in His heart through a clarion call. The prophet releases words, thoughts, messages and inspirations that are beating in the heart of God right now.

What is *prophetic intercession*? It is where the ministry of the priest and prophet unite. A passage in Jeremiah says it wonderfully: "If they are prophets, and if the word of the LORD is with them, let them now entreat the LORD of hosts" (Jeremiah

27:18). Prophetic intercessors do not only pronounce the word of the Lord; they in turn pray the promise back to the Father! In so doing they actually give birth to the promise.

Prophetic intercession, therefore, paves the way for the fulfillment of the prophetic promise. It also assumes the larger boundaries of the purposes of God. Prophetic intercession does not merely ask that people make right decisions for Christ, it does it within the larger boundaries of the great purposes of God.

In other words, as prophetic intercessors, we plead for the maturity of Christ in those who respond, praying that the new society of redeemed humankind may expand unto the ends of the earth. Whether prophetic intercession is preached truth, prayed burden or spontaneous utterance, it is only truly prophetic if it brings its hearers, its generation, into the knowledge of the heart of God for their time.

### How Does Prophetic Intercession Work?

In prophetic intercession the Spirit of God pleads the covenant promises made throughout history to be enacted in our day. This inspired form of intercession is the urge to pray, given by the Holy Spirit, for a situation or circumstance about which you may have little natural knowledge. But you are praying the prayer request that is on the heart of God. He nudges you to pray so that He can intervene. The Holy Spirit Himself directs you to pray in a divine manner to bring forth His will on earth as it already is in heaven.

In other words, prophetic intercession is the ability to receive a prayer request from God and pray it back to Him. God's hand comes on you, and He imparts His burden to you. Prophetic intercession is not as much *praying to God* as it is *praying with God*! Oh my! What a difference! Your God-inspired, God-directed intercession is powerful and effective.

Prophetic intercessors do not take those little plastic "promise boxes" with Bible verses inside and randomly select a verse to pray through. Instead, they combine waiting, listening and reading the Scriptures with letting the Holy Spirit remind them of the particular promise that is on His heart at that moment. They let God's heartbeat pulse in their own beings.

Prophetic intercession pleads for the maturity of the Body of Christ—that the society of redeemed mankind would expand to the ends of the earth. It is the place where the priest and prophet unite, calling "for the earth [to] be filled with the knowledge of the glory of the LORD, as the waters cover the sea" (Habakkuk 2:14).

Prophetic intercession does not always take place in a prayer room. As a believer receives a burden from the Lord, which can happen anyplace, he or she responds by expressing this back to Him. Sometimes this is accompanied or followed by distinct actions before God, others and the world, as well as appropriate declarations to block hosts of darkness from their diabolical aspirations.

### "To Breathe Together"

Ours is the privilege of entering into the actual intercession of Christ, yielding ourselves to Him so that He can flow through us. In prayer we become laborers with Christ and enter into partnership with the Creator of the universe!

The burden of prophetic intercession begins as a flame and grows into a consuming fire as the revelation concerning the purposes of God for our generation increases. It might start as an inner conviction of His will, a sudden awareness of His nearness or hearing of a situation that triggers a spiritual response.

All prophetic intercession carries the struggle of birth. The heart of the intercessor becomes the womb in which God's prophetic purposes come forth. In this place the struggle between old traditions and new ways takes place. We become the hand-maidens of the Lord in whom the "new and old wineskins" collide. As we hear God's voice, we become convinced that a radical revolution of the Christian faith is near. The prophetic intercessor conspires with God that His glory will be seen, felt and known in the earth.

The word *conspire* means literally "to breathe together." It expresses the most intimate joining of life. When God created man from the dust of the earth, He "breathed into his nostrils the breath of life; and man became a living being" (Genesis 2:7). This Hebrew word translated *breathed* can mean "to breathe violently." Such was the occasion when there was the sound of a violent wind filling the Upper Room as God sent His Spirit upon and into His newborn Church.

Prophetic intercession is our conspiring together with God, "breathing violently" into situations through prayer to bring forth life. When God's people receive the spirit of grace and supplication (see Zechariah 12:10), they share a sense of divine possibility and excitement. God shatters their old expectations.

### Three Definitions of Prophetic Intercession

Here, to summarize what I have presented above, are three definitions of prophetic intercession:

1. Prophetic intercession is the ability to receive an immediate prayer request from God and pray about it in a divinely anointed utterance.

2. Prophetic intercession is waiting before God in order to "hear" or receive God's burden (God's Word, His concern, warning, conditions, vision or promises), responding back to the Lord and then to the people with appropriate actions.

3. Prophetic intercession is not as much praying to God as it is praying with God. We let go of our agendas and we take the time to receive the desires that are in God's heart. Thus, prophetic intercession (revelatory prayer) is praying *with* God!

### Scriptural Guidelines for Prophetic Intercession

In one Scripture after another, the Holy Spirit reveals how He works with prophetic people within intercession. Some of these principles we have covered already, such as the idea contained within James 2:1 that prophetic intercessors must not criticize or call down judgment, but rather pray with a heart full of mercy and compassion.

Read these familiar passages with fresh understanding:

My brethren, do not hold your faith in our glorious Lord Jesus Christ with an attitude of personal favoritism.

James 2:1

Surely the LORD God does nothing, unless He reveals His secret to His servants the prophets.

Amos 3:7 NKJV

We are only God's coworkers. You are God's garden, not ours; you are God's building, not ours.

1 Corinthians 3:9 TLB

Now to Him who is able to do exceedingly abundantly above all that we ask or think, according to the power that works in us.

Ephesians 3:20 NKJV

Likewise the Spirit also helps in our weaknesses. For we do not know what we should pray for as we ought, but the Spirit

Himself makes intercession for us with groanings which cannot be uttered.

Romans 8:26 NKJV

For from days of old they have not heard or perceived by ear, nor has the eye seen a God besides You, who acts in behalf of the one who waits for Him.

Isaiah 64:4

There is another way of interceding that is scripturally validated by the story of Abraham "bartering" with God over the fate of Sodom and Gomorrah:

The LORD said, "The outcry of Sodom and Gomorrah is indeed great, and their sin is exceedingly grave. I will go down now, and see if they have done entirely according to its outcry, which has come to Me; and if not, I will know."
... Abraham came near and said, "Will You indeed sweep away the righteous with the wicked? Suppose there are fifty righteous within the city; will You indeed sweep it away and not spare the place for the sake of the fifty righteous who are in it? Far be it from You to do such a thing, to slay the righteous with the wicked, so that the righteous and the wicked are treated alike. Far be it from You! Shall not the Judge of all the earth deal justly?" So the LORD said, "If I find in Sodom fifty righteous within the city, then I will spare the whole place on their account." And Abraham replied, "Now behold, I have ventured to speak to the LORD, although I am but dust and ashes. Suppose the fifty righteous are lacking five, will You destroy the whole city because of five?" And He said, "I will not destroy it if I find forty-five there." He spoke to Him yet again and said, "Suppose forty are found there?" And He said, "I will not do it on account of the forty." Then he said, "Oh may the LORD not be angry, and I shall speak; suppose thirty are found there?" And He said, "I will not do it if I find thirty there." And he said, "Now behold, I have ventured to speak to the

LORD; suppose twenty are found there?" And He said, "I will not destroy it on account of the twenty." Then he said, "Oh may the LORD not be angry, and I shall speak only this once; suppose ten are found there?" And He said, "I will not destroy it on account of the ten."

Genesis 18:20–21, 23–32

Abraham is banking on the fact that God's mercy triumphs over judgment. How else would he dare to counter God's righteous judgment on the wicked cities? He makes appeal after appeal, lowering the count of righteous souls each time. God never stops him, does He? He never says, "That's enough. Get out of My way." God stops listening to Abraham's appeals only when Abraham stops making them.

This shows us something very interesting about God's heart of love: *God quits when man quits,* at least where intercessory negotiations are concerned. He wants to show as much mercy as possible, even in an extreme situation, and He wants to involve His intercessors with His heart of mercy.

### Receiving and Responding to the Burden of the Lord

God may quit when we quit praying, but He is the one who initiates the praying in the first place. Often it comes when we recall a promise that He has made in the past, something for which the time of fulfillment has come. That is what we see in the book of Daniel. In the book of Jeremiah's prophecies, Daniel observed that a specified number of years had been tallied, and that it was soon going to be time for God to act on behalf of His people:

In the first year of Darius the son of Ahasuerus, of Median descent, who was made king over the kingdom of the Chaldeans—in the first year of his reign, I, Daniel, observed in the books the number of the years which was revealed as the word of the LORD to Jeremiah the prophet for the completion of the desolations of Jerusalem, namely, seventy years.

*Daniel 9:1–2*

Here is what Daniel read in the book of Jeremiah's prophecies:

For thus says the LORD, "When seventy years have been completed for Babylon, I will visit you and fulfill My good word to you, to bring you back to this place."

*Jeremiah 29:10*

Daniel began to pray, with divine guidance, through the promises that had been given to the earlier generation, zeroing in on the ones that had not yet been fulfilled. The underlying promise was that at the end of seventy years, the people would be released from Babylonian captivity. Daniel, therefore, in a spirit of prophetically informed intercession, prayed from the midst of his own captivity in Babylon with conviction and discernment and humility, ending his prayers with these words:

So now, our God, listen to the prayer of Your servant and to his supplications, and for Your sake, O Lord, let Your face shine on Your desolate sanctuary. O my God, incline Your ear and hear! Open Your eyes and see our desolations and the city which is called by Your name; for we are not presenting our supplications before You on account of any merits of our own, but on account of Your great compassion. O Lord, hear! O Lord, forgive! O Lord, listen and take action! For Your own sake, O my God, do not delay, because Your city and Your people are called by Your name.

*Daniel 9:17–19*

Because of his prayers, the hindrances that were in the way of the fulfillment of the promise were removed, although not without difficulty. As he expected, the children of Israel began to be released from their exile at the seventy-year mark. The prophetic promise was fulfilled—but only because Daniel prayed so long and well.

It appears to be vital that the guiding prophetic word be written down or recorded in some way. Daniel had Jeremiah's written word. The prophet Habakkuk addressed the idea directly:

> The burden which the prophet Habakkuk saw . . . I will stand my watch and set myself on the rampart, and watch to see what He will say to me, and what I will answer when I am corrected. Then the LORD answered me and said:
>
> "Write the vision and make it plain on tablets, that he may run who reads it. For the vision is yet for an appointed time; but at the end it will speak, and it will not lie. Though it tarries, wait for it; because it will surely come, it will not tarry."
>
> Habakkuk 1:1; 2:1–3 NKJV

This is good advice for us today. We need to learn to journal as part of our prophetic intercession. By quieting ourselves before the Lord, we can lay hold of what He is saying to us. By writing it down for future reference, we can find guidance for our prayers when the time is right. I am in the midst of the praying part of this exercise right now. I wrote down some prophetic words thirty years ago, and I believe that it is now time for them to be fulfilled. Without my journals to look back on, I would have forgotten. With the journals, I can see what the Spirit may be highlighting to my attention, and then I can start to pray as He leads about what He told me decades ago.

It will be different each time and with each person. As with any gift, there are various levels of operation within the sphere of prophecy. There can be the *occasional gift* that empowers an individual for a specific situation. There can be a further stage of development in which there is a more consistent flow of *prophetic operation* as the believer matures. Some are blessed to enjoy a more consistent *prophetic ministry*, but this does not necessarily mean the individual has an Ephesians 4:11 *office of prophet.* Only God can bring someone to this level of consistent grace that blooms over time, with training. At some point, after consistent fruit and recognition from leaders, a person may be officially commissioned into the prophetic calling. In whatever manner the process unfolds, gifts are given but fruit is borne over time. Gifts may appear overnight, but character is necessary to steward them. Character comes only by way of the cross, and good, ripe fruit requires time, exposed to the Son.

### Responding to the Burden of the Lord

I cannot overstress the importance of growing in maturity, which only happens as you walk responsively with the Lord over time. Nobody knows how to do this at first; you must learn as you go.

For your heart to beat the same as God's heart, you need to cultivate a humble awareness of your position as a child of the Father, loved passionately but weak and submissive as well. Especially when you start proclaiming promises and claiming territory for God, remember to stick to your sphere of authority. Watch out for self-righteousness and secret pride. Take your cues from the Spirit Himself, not from other believers, past or present.

Learn how to "plead your case" before the throne as in a court of law, handling all of the evidence with care and respect. The most powerful plea you can bring before the throne is the shed blood of His Son. The devil, the flesh and the world will do their best (i.e., worst) to deter you, but their objections cannot stand when you "plead the blood of Christ."

The famous preacher Charles Spurgeon wrote:

> Do not reckon you have prayed unless you have pleaded, for pleading is the very marrow of prayer. He who pleads well knows the secret of prevailing with God, especially if he pleads the blood of Jesus, for that unlocks the treasury of heaven. Many keys fit many locks, but the master key is the blood and the name of Him that died and rose again, and ever lives in heaven to save unto the uttermost.[1]

It never hurts to testify about what the blood of Christ has done for you personally. This is the psalmist's exhortation: "Let the redeemed of the LORD say so, whom He has redeemed from the hand of the enemy" (Psalm 107:2 NKJV).

The blood of Christ is utterly persuasive. Why? On the Day of Atonement, an Old Testament high priest would go from the altar of incense to the most holy place that lay beyond the thick veil. Putting blood from the sacrificed bull or goat on his finger, he would sprinkle it seven times on the mercy seat and on the horns of the altar. Only the high priest could enter the holy of holies, and only on that one day of the year—and even so he could not gain access to God's holy presence without that sacrificial blood.

Today, however, since the coming of Jesus and His sacrificial death and resurrection, we "high priests" bring His blood when we come before the throne of our holy God:

> You have come . . . to God, the Judge of all, and to the spirits of the righteous made perfect, and to Jesus, the mediator of a new covenant, and to the sprinkled blood, which speaks better than the blood of Abel.
>
> Hebrews 12:22–24

Jesus' blood "speaks better than the blood of Abel" because He was even more innocent of sin than Abel was. Abel, you will remember, was murdered by his brother Cain. The innocent blood of Abel cried out from the ground so that God heard it and responded to its cry. How much more clearly does the pure blood of the crucified Son of God speak into the Father's ears?

From the ground, Jesus' blood cries out for justice but also for mercy. Just think of how many ways His blood was shed, even before He reached the cross: (1) In Gethsemane, "being in agony, He prayed more earnestly. Then His sweat became like great drops of blood falling down to the ground" (Luke 22:44 NKJV); (2) after His arrest, he was struck with rods and then scourged (see Matthew 26:63–67; 27:26); (3) the soldiers pressed the crown of thorns into His scalp (see Matthew 27:29); (4) His hands and feet were nailed to the cross (see Matthew 27:35); (5) as His blood was already dripping to the ground at the base of the cross, the soldier pierced His side with a spear (see John 19:34).

His blood was not shed in vain. By testifying to what the blood of Jesus has accomplished, we enforce His triumph over the powers of darkness. His blood itself cries out and intercedes for us, and the more we declare its benefits, the more clearly that cry arises. In John's revelation, we see that "they [the believers] overcame him [the accuser of the brethren, Satan] because of the blood of the Lamb and because of the word of their testimony, and they did not love their life even when faced with death" (Revelation 12:11).

When you are grappling in prayer with a burden that originates with the Lord, you can ask Him to shine His light on the path you should take. Most of the time, it will lead you straight to the foot of the cross.

Our God wants us to come to Him like this. He said so through the prophet Isaiah (here in three different versions to bring out the highlights):

> Put Me in remembrance, let us argue our case together; state your cause, that you may be proved right.
>
> Isaiah 43:26 NASB

Put Me in remembrance; let us contend together; state your case, that you may be acquitted.

NKJV

Oh, remind me of this promise of forgiveness, for we must talk about your sins. Plead your case for my forgiving you.

TLB

## Where Are My Daniels and Esthers?

Some years ago I took a train from Heidelberg to Rosenheim, Germany—a six-hour journey in the middle of the night. While attempting to rest on the train, I kept hearing the gentle voice of the Holy Spirit. I know He was talking to me as an individual, but He was also imparting a burden for prayer.

Here is what I heard Him speak:

*Where are My Daniels? Where are My Esthers? Where are My Deborahs? And where are My Josephs?*

As the train pressed through the darkness, *clack-clack-clack-clack*, I kept hearing His piercing, relentless plea:

*Where are My Daniels? Where are My Esthers? Where are My Deborahs? And where are My Josephs?*

I close out this strategic chapter, then, with this plea. I am convinced that you, reading this book right now, were created "for such a time as this" (Esther 4:14). For such a prophetic intercessory task, God brought *you* forth. Will you arise and be one of His radical revolutionaries? Will you be one of the answers to His persistent plea?

It is not too late to answer the call, to volunteer for on-the-job training and to be commissioned as one of God's servant-warriors. I think I can hear drumbeats in the background. The march is beginning as humble, persistent warriors are aligning themselves under God's command. Now I can hear another sound coming forth: "Calling all watchmen! The time has come for you to mount your walls. Prophetic intercessors arise!"

## A Prophetic Appeal for Intercession

In closing, I would like to present to you a portion of a relevant prophetic word given by one of the Church statesmen of our day, Jack Hayford, chancellor emeritus of The King's University, former senior pastor of Church On The Way in Van Nuys, California, and the fourth president of the International Church of the Foursquare Gospel. Although the word was delivered August 1, 1980, it is yet one of the clearest trumpet sounds I have ever heard and worthy of our review:

> The Lord God would call all of His redeemed in this land to lift up their eyes and look! Over your nation there are leaden skies, clouds of impending judgment which hang heavy with a rain of fury and indignation which this people have brought upon themselves. As sin has risen as a vapor of evil, now clouds of judgment have formed and shall shortly be precipitated in wrath and destruction, except an intercessor rise to hold back the storm.
>
> And so the Lord calls: O Church, cause your words to rise in prayers of intercession unto deliverance. The skies are dropping lower, skies of lead weighted with judgment, but your entry with prayer can save the day. For the Lord would have you see that your intercession, O Church, rises like pillars, extending through prayer and pressing back the impending judgment, pushing the leaden skies upward and backward. Take your place as pillars of prayer, for I would that there be mercy upon this nation rather than judgment; I would there be healing rather than death!
>
> Cause the word to go forth with understanding that My people need not surrender to the storm which threatens. Did I not deliver Nineveh when repentance came? If you pray

ceaselessly until the leaden skies of judgment be lifted by pillars of prayer, then will the light, the glory and the blessing of the Lord flood your land and healing come again. Lift up your voices with praise, raising pillars of intercession, and you shall see the deliverance of God, if you will pray as He directs.[2]

Read it again and see if you do not agree that it throbs with the heartbeat of God. Allow God's words to move you to present yourself to Him as one of His intercessors who will shoulder His burdens in prayer as we move into the dark days ahead.

### Prayer to Have God's Heart

Father, in the mighty name of the Son of God, I ask that You will bring my heart into union with Yours so that it can beat with the burdens and desires that are in Your heart. Give me both an increase of the Spirit of revelation and the supernatural authority to stand in the gap in Christ's name. Like Anna, I want to pray Your prophetic promises into being. Amen.

# 10

# Proclamation

## Decreeing a Thing

*O*ur assignment as prophetic intercessors makes us watchmen who not only scan the horizon for potential dangers but also those who proclaim the authority of God loud and clear.

This was brought home to me forcefully one day when I was alone, waiting quietly upon the Lord, and the voice of the Holy Spirit came to me saying, "It is time to make a worldwide impact by calling forth the watchmen to the prophetic power of proclamation."

"The prophetic power of proclamation"—this was like the final piece of the puzzle for me, and it shifted me into ministering out of a higher vision from that point forward.

### Watchmen on the Walls

The picture was clear to me, because I had seen it in the book of Isaiah:

> On your walls, O Jerusalem, I have appointed watchmen; all day and all night they will never keep silent. You who remind the LORD, take no rest for yourselves; and give Him no rest until He establishes and makes Jerusalem a praise in the earth.
>
> Isaiah 62:6–7

To state the obvious—if we are up on top of the walls being watchmen, we are not down on the ground observing and participating in whatever is happening on the horizontal plane. We stay up high at our posts, because that is the only way to get an overview. As watchman-intercessors, the height of our revelation will determine our perspective.

If we watchmen on the walls will never be silent day or night, what are we saying while we are up there? We are reminding God of His Word—the promises and proclamations of Scripture as well as the current promises that are in the Father's heart today. It is as though we have been issued megaphones so that we can echo God's Word to the world around us.

We find that there is more than one way to dismantle the darkness around us. It is not always by firing arrows or using other weapons. More often, it is by proclaiming God's blessings, which supplant the curses that afflict the people and the territory we have been charged to watch over. Blessings and praises proclaimed wholeheartedly will break the power of a curse better than addressing it directly with a rebuke. "Bless those who persecute you; bless and do not curse" (Romans 12:14). The power of a blessing is greater than the power of a curse.

As watchmen on the walls, our job is to pray God's promises, to praise Him with our whole hearts and to release proclamations of prophetic blessings. As we do so, we ourselves will grow increasingly secure in our identity as sons and daughters of the Father. That increased security will keep us from breaking out in our own effort to do prayer "exploits" that are too ambitious and self-serving—while the results of our prayers and proclamations may at times surprise us with joy.

## Healing in Bangkok

Let me give you a clear example of how this works.

I was ministering in meetings in Bangkok, Thailand, where literal curses abound. During the daytime series of teachings, through a translator, I did a rather methodical presentation about the causes and cures for curses. Among other things, I pointed out that Jesus addressed demons directly in the course of His ministry. The material I taught was well received.

But when the subsequent time of ministry came, I did not follow the typical individual personal ministry approach. Through a series of dreams beforehand, the Holy Spirit had shown me a different way. I started releasing the "opposite spirit," the spirit of blessing, over the assembled crowd. No one laid hands on anybody else. I led the people in corporate declarations of blessings and the faith level began to go up. Everyone was eagerly participating together. That afternoon session ended with expectation for more at the closing evening meeting.

That evening during the time of worship, a lady started dancing her way across the front. I did not know what was so special about that, but people were reacting excitedly. I turned to my interpreter. "What is happening?" and he said, "Oh, don't you know?" He explained to me that this was the woman who had been in the earlier teaching meeting. She had come in desperate need, because her whole right side was paralyzed. Apparently she had been going to doctor after doctor, but no one had been able to help her. She was ready to have one more MRI the following week, but she was getting resigned to a lifetime of major paralysis.

That afternoon, with no one laying hands on her, she had confessed and renounced some generational sins as I had instructed. Then when I started releasing the power of the blessings, she got struck by a "lightning bolt" of Holy Spirit power and she was healed in an instant. That night she was offering thanks to God by doing what she could not do before—dance. She was completely healed!

Now, we do not always see such dramatic results, but I can tell you that if the proclamation of God's word of blessing is strong enough to heal paralysis, it is definitely strong enough to heal whatever else might be out of order. I recommend it highly!

### Proclaim for All to Hear

We do not use the words "proclaim" or "proclamation" often in our ordinary speech. We prefer synonymous words such as "announce" or "publish" or "invite" or "declare." Let's revive *proclamation* as one of our best ways of being prophetic intercessors. Let's "cry out," "pronounce," "herald," or even, as in the title of this chapter, "decree."

We speak in behalf of the King, do we not? As His own sons and daughters, we can proclaim God's truth with joyful confidence in any situation.

Just look at this collection of proclamatory Scriptures!

> I will proclaim the name of the LORD. Oh, praise the greatness of our God! He is the Rock, his works are perfect, and all his ways are just. A faithful God who does no wrong, upright and just is he.
>
> Deuteronomy 32:3–4 NIV

> The Spirit of the Sovereign LORD is on me, because the LORD has anointed me to proclaim good news to the poor. He has sent me to bind up the brokenhearted, to proclaim freedom for the captives and release from darkness for the prisoners, to proclaim the year of the LORD's favor and the day of vengeance of our God,

to comfort all who mourn, and provide for those who grieve in Zion—to bestow on them a crown of beauty instead of ashes, the oil of joy instead of mourning, and a garment of praise instead of a spirit of despair. They will be called oaks of righteousness, a planting of the LORD for the display of his splendor.

Isaiah 61:1–3 NIV

What I tell you in the darkness, speak in the light; and what you hear whispered in your ear, proclaim upon the housetops.

Matthew 10:27

So, having obtained help from God, I stand to this day testifying both to small and great, stating nothing but what the Prophets and Moses said was going to take place; that the Christ was to suffer, and that by reason of His resurrection from the dead He would be the first to proclaim light both to the Jewish people and to the Gentiles.

Acts 26:22–23

What was from the beginning, what we have heard, what we have seen with our eyes, what we have looked at and touched with our hands, concerning the Word of Life—and the life was manifested, and we have seen and testify and proclaim to you the eternal life, which was with the Father and was manifested to us—what we have seen and heard we proclaim to you also, so that you too may have fellowship with us; and indeed our fellowship is with the Father, and with His Son Jesus Christ.

1 John 1:1–3

We not only cry out our proclamations, but we also sing psalms and hymns and spiritual songs—to each other:

Talk with each other much about the Lord, quoting psalms and hymns and singing sacred songs, making music in your hearts to the Lord.

Ephesians 5:19 TLB

Let the message of Christ dwell among you richly as you teach and admonish one another with all wisdom through psalms, hymns, and songs from the Spirit, singing to God with gratitude in your hearts.

Colossians 3:16 NIV

## "Thereby good will come to you"

We can learn much from the counsel that was given to Job:

Yield now and be at peace with Him; thereby good will come to you. Please receive instruction from His mouth and establish His words in your heart. If you return to the Almighty, you will be restored; if you remove unrighteousness far from your tent, and place your gold in the dust, and the gold of Ophir among the stones of the brooks, then the Almighty will be your gold and choice silver to you. For then you will delight in the Almighty and lift up your face to God. You will pray to Him, and He will hear you; and you will pay your vows. You will also decree a thing, and it will be established for you; and light will shine on your ways.

Job 22:21–28

Here is the progression: First, there is a confession of sin, followed by the intentional removing of obstacles. Then as you establish the Word of God in your heart, you secure your heart of submission. This enables you to receive instruction and to repent and return to the Lord. Your guiding revelation will be that God is your all in all and your delight, which will cause you to remove all of your former idols and do everything you promised Him.

Then and only then—after you have met all of these conditions—will you be able to "decree a thing and it will be established for you; and light will shine on your ways."

People quote that verse often and they claim it, but they fail to read what comes before it. Then they wonder why their proclamatory prayers fail to secure results. They fail to confess their own sin (and the sin of the people for whom they may be praying). They fail to perform what I call "process praying," in which each step builds on the one before.

## The Proclamation of Praise

You may wonder what praise has to do with proclamation.

Well, everything. Remember how speaking and singing psalms and hymns and spiritual songs works. Remember how effective it is to decree prophetic destiny and purpose and to speak blessings instead of aligning with the darkness.

As watchmen, we take the high view. As prophetic intercessors, we reach higher. "Higher" means heaven. And the promise of the proclamation of praise is that it takes you up to God's habitation.

Do you want to establish a throne over your family, your home, your city, your church, your ministry, your nation where Jesus comes and sits in all of His authority? You can build such a throne through your high praises: "You are holy, O You who are enthroned upon the praises of Israel" (Psalm 22:3).

Praise sanctifies the atmosphere; it opens the way to God's presence: "Enter His gates with thanksgiving and His courts with praise. Give thanks to Him, bless His name" (Psalm 100:4). The results befit a well-established watchman:

> No longer will violence be heard in your land, nor ruin or destruction within your borders, but you will call your walls Salvation and your gates Praise.
>
> Isaiah 60:18 NIV

Praise becomes like a garment for your spirit:

171

To grant those who mourn in Zion, giving them a garland instead of ashes, the oil of gladness instead of mourning, the mantle of praise instead of a spirit of fainting. So they will be called oaks of righteousness, the planting of the LORD, that He may be glorified.

Isaiah 61:3

Praise lifts up God's glory, and it draws down heavenly holiness, authority and provision. Unlikely as it seems, it therefore becomes a weapon of spiritual warfare, a means of deliverance. Psalm 50:23 states it outright: "He who offers a sacrifice of thanksgiving honors Me; and to him who orders his way aright I shall show the salvation of God."

### Examples of Effective Praise

God-ordained praise is powerful indeed. It will silence Satan and put a stop to his schemes:

Out of the mouth of babes and nursing infants You have ordained strength, because of Your enemies, that You may silence the enemy and the avenger.

Psalm 8:2 NKJV

Praise changes hearts and brings the Kingdom of God to earth. It brings restoration:

"The voice of joy and the voice of gladness, the voice of the bridegroom and the voice of the bride, the voice of those who say, 'Give thanks to the LORD of hosts, for the LORD is good, for His lovingkindness is everlasting'; and of those who bring a thank offering into the house of the LORD. For I will restore the fortunes of the land as they were at first," says the LORD.

Jeremiah 33:11

Paul and Silas were set free from prison miraculously as they declared the praises of God with enthusiasm:

But about midnight Paul and Silas were praying and singing hymns of praise to God, and the prisoners were listening to them; and suddenly there came a great earthquake, so that the foundations of the prison house were shaken; and immediately all the doors were opened and everyone's chains were unfastened.

Acts 16:25–26

Jonah was set free from prison, too—the prison of the belly of the big fish—by praising God and surrendering to His sovereignty:

Then Jonah prayed to the Lord his God from the stomach of the fish, and he said,
"I called out of my distress to the LORD, and He answered me. I cried for help from the depth of Sheol; You heard my voice. For You had cast me into the deep, into the heart of the seas, and the current engulfed me. All Your breakers and billows passed over me. So I said, 'I have been expelled from Your sight. Nevertheless I will look again toward Your holy temple.' Water encompassed me to the point of death. The great deep engulfed me, weeds were wrapped around my head. I descended to the roots of the mountains. The earth with its bars was around me forever, but You have brought up my life from the pit, O LORD my God. While I was fainting away, I remembered the LORD, and my prayer came to You, into Your holy temple. Those who regard vain idols forsake their faithfulness, but I will sacrifice to You with the voice of thanksgiving. That which I have vowed I will pay. Salvation is from the LORD."
Then the LORD commanded the fish, and it vomited Jonah up onto the dry land.

Jonah 2:1–10

### Examples of the Power of Proclamation

One of the clearest examples of the power of proclamation is the well-known story of David and Goliath (see 1 Samuel

17:43–51). We remember how at first King Saul suited up David with his own unwieldy armor and sword, which David abandoned quickly in favor of his most familiar weapons, a simple sling and five smooth stones from the bed of the brook. Then he stepped forward and made a public declaration. Using clear words, he proclaimed to the strongman, Goliath, as well as to the assembled warriors from both sides:

> You come to me with a sword, a spear, and a javelin, but I come to you in the name of the LORD of hosts, the God of the armies of Israel, whom you have taunted. This day the LORD will deliver you up into my hands, and I will strike you down and remove your head from you. And I will give the dead bodies of the army of the Philistines this day to the birds of the sky and the wild beasts of the earth, that all the earth may know that there is a God in Israel, and that all this assembly may know that the LORD does not deliver by sword or by spear; for the battle is the LORD's and He will give you into our hands.
>
> 1 Samuel 17:45–47

Proclaiming that he was a representative of One who was greater, and disregarding the fact that he was a mere teenager standing there in his own shepherd's clothing, he selected one of the stones and flung it toward his fierce adversary quicker than anybody could react. He had four more stones, but he did not need them, because the first one did the trick. It sank into the forehead of the giant and killed him. The strongman was down for the count and the army of Israel declared victory.

This is the power of proclamation. "You come to me with a sword, a spear, and a javelin, but I come to you in the name of the LORD of hosts," thus defeating the spiritual hosts of wickedness that were motivating the Philistines to trample the people of God.

When God called Gideon forward to fight with confidence, He sent an angel to make the proclamation that would set the reluctant warrior on his feet:

Then the angel of the LORD came and sat under the oak that was in Ophrah, which belonged to Joash the Abiezrite as his son Gideon was beating out wheat in the wine press in order to save it from the Midianites. The angel of the LORD appeared to him and said to him, "The LORD is with you, O valiant warrior." Then Gideon said to him, "O my lord, if the LORD is with us, why then has all this happened to us? And where are all His miracles which our fathers told us about, saying, 'Did not the LORD bring us up from Egypt?' But now the LORD has abandoned us and given us into the hand of Midian." The LORD looked at him and said, "Go in this your strength and deliver Israel from the hand of Midian. Have I not sent you?"

Judges 6:11–14

Gideon did not consider himself to be a mighty warrior who was in any way qualified or fortified for such an assignment. God's angel used the power of proclamation to put strength into him.

These stories are so familiar to us that we miss the dynamics that are meant to teach us how to pray. Another example is the story of Joshua and the city of Jericho (see Joshua 6). Here God began by bringing the people into unity. They had been grumbling, complaining, bickering and fighting among themselves. God's instrument of discipline was the command to march *silently* around the city of Jericho. He put a zipper on their mouths and after enough marching their silence formed them into a responsive unit that was capable of obeying His next command faultlessly—shout out!

Joshua commanded the people, saying, "You shall not shout nor let your voice be heard nor let a word proceed out of your mouth, until the day I tell you, 'Shout!' Then you shall shout!"

Joshua 6:10

175

The shout of proclamation released the city from the enemy's grip and placed it into the hands of God's people. With the walls shattered, the completion of the defeat was assured.

## Proclaim and Decree

The gentleman who has affected my life more than anyone except Jesus Himself is Derek Prince, whose long ministry as a Bible teacher is legendary. On a regular basis, he would lead people in the following Scripture-based proclamation:[1]

1. Through the blood of Jesus, I am redeemed out of the hand of the devil.
2. Through the blood of Jesus, all my sins are forgiven.
3. The blood of Jesus Christ, God's Son, continually cleanses me from all sin.
4. Through the blood of Jesus, I am justified, made righteous, just-as-if-I'd-never sinned.
5. Through the blood of Jesus, I am sanctified, made holy, set apart to God.
6. My body is a temple of the Holy Spirit, redeemed, cleansed by the blood of Jesus.
7. Satan has no place in me, no power over me, through the blood of Jesus!

There is no deeper truth than Jesus Christ, crucified and risen from the dead. We can cleanse ourselves with the blood of Jesus, washing ourselves clean with words. The authoritative words we proclaim as part of our effective prayers come directly from God Himself, and they elevate us into His presence.

Instead of only "praying problems," we proclaim solutions.

Each time you and I proclaim the power of God over our lives and over the lives of the people around us, the statement

I made at the beginning of the chapter comes to fruition: "It is time to make a worldwide impact by calling forth the watchmen to the prophetic power of proclamation." Let's make full use of the power of proclamation. Let's decree things, and see them established. Let's fill our mouths with vigorous words of praise and we will see whole cities transformed for the glory of God!

## Decreeing a Thing and Seeing It Established

Father God, grant me a higher revelation of how to enter into effective spiritual warfare through the power of proclamation. Holy Spirit, teach me how to release God's solutions instead of only praying man's problems. Fill my heart and mouth with the power of praise and join my prayers with others' so that we can see whole cities transformed for the glory of God! Amen.

# 11

# Wisdom for Intercessors

At various times in my life I have asked for the power of God to set captives free. (I still do.) I have cried out for finances to be able to extend His Kingdom. (I still need this, too.) On other occasions I have pleaded for the holiness of God. (I am still desperate for this.) Many times I have sought the Lord for a compassionate and merciful heart. (I continue to pursue this as well.)

There seems to be no end to the list of things we need from God. Yet, we must learn to pray for the long haul, instead of just coming out with the occasional brilliant prayer that bursts forth like a Roman candle shooting up into the night only to fizzle out as quickly as it flared up.

If I were given only one thing to ask for, I would follow the example of King Solomon and request wisdom for my life journey. It is the single most vital ingredient necessary for the long haul. I will continue to lift up one of the three Spirit-inspired prayers from my youth—"Give me wisdom beyond my years."

I know that I need wisdom more today than I did yesterday, and I will surely need more tomorrow than I do today.

## Listen to the Commander in Chief

Although I have never served on active military duty, I have fought in many "air" wars. I have spent sleepless nights watching and waiting for orders from my Commander in Chief, on the alert for whatever was needed next. I have spent days fasting, not only because of Jesus' worthiness but because I was desperate for help or my heart was breaking for someone.

The Christian life is not just about wine and roses, intimate times and hangin' with Jesus. The romance of being part of the Bride of Christ may be preferable, but that is not all there is. We need to be the fighting Bride (see Ephesians 5:25–27; 6:13–18). We must hold tightly onto God's hand (intimacy) while moving out with His authority (warfare). It is not one or the other; the intimacy enables us to war effectively. As the title of one of Francis Frangipane's books aptly declares, "This day we fight!"

It takes guts to serve in the military; it is a tough duty. We need courage. When you hit the enemy, he likes to hit back. One of the tricks for surviving battles is to be like a rhinoceros with a thick skin and a big heart. I do not have that one down yet. Many of us, in fact, tend to be either hard-hearted or thin-skinned. But wisdom helps. As we grow in wisdom, we learn to be both tough and tender even as we learn how to heed implicitly the voice of our Commander in Chief.

Every believer in Christ Jesus is called to be a changemaker before the throne of God by fulfilling our priestly functions of worship, prayer, praise and intercession. None of these functions requires a special spiritual gift, because everybody is expected to perform them. In Scripture, there is no spiritual gift called "spiritual warfare" and there is not a gift called "prayer" or "intercession." These are simply part of our standard equipment. I like to say that God is an equal opportunity Employer.

As a believer, every single one of us has the privilege of ministering directly to Him. It goes beyond your other gifts and callings. It does not depend upon your geographical location. It pays no attention to your economic status. Worship, prayer, praise, intercession. And if we are attentive to His voice, that intercession becomes prophetic.

As prayer warriors, we find that we combat the demonic powers of darkness on different levels, depending on our assignments in the Kingdom. Several streams of teaching emphasize the levels differently. Some advocate what you could call aggressive intercession or confrontational intercession. They teach about spiritual warfare in the heavenly realm and earthly territorial spirits more than personal deliverance ministry.

Others take a more moderate approach, or even a conservative one. The important thing is not a particular approach as much as it is being aware of the dynamics and potential of prayer engagement. You may end up on assignments behind the scenes, but you will need to support the role of the Special Forces.

## Wisdom Lessons for Intercessors

Where do we as intercessors and soldiers begin? We may recognize the importance of wisdom. We may even love and desire it. But how do we actually obtain it? Far too often believers ask God for wisdom only to get in way over their heads. That is why we find the highways of spiritual warfare littered with casualties. If we push forward, ignoring warning signals and signs, we can easily end up in a ditch or stalled along the roadside, burned out for Jesus, overheated and exhausted.

I have been around this mountain a few times myself, and have seen many people running like hamsters on a wheel of misfortune. I have learned a lot the hard way. Now I want to share some lessons I am learning regarding the pitfalls and perils of intercessory warfare.

God will give us wisdom if we ask Him (see James 1:5), but like good soldiers in training, we have to learn how to use it. I can think of ten distinct wisdom applications for intercessors, and I want to spend some time on each one of them.

### 1. Get a Life!

Too often it seems that people involved in prophetic, intercessory and spiritual warfare get so engaged in the seriousness of their task that they miss the joy of common, everyday living. Some of us try so hard to discern every breeze or to interpret the significance of every bird that flies by the window that we become granola Christians—nutty, flaky and fruity!

My basic counsel is, get a life. Go for a walk; it will help your soul. Find a hobby; it will do you good. Go work out at the gym; get some exercise and release the tension. Your physical body will thank you and others might like you better. Take care of yourself—rest, exercise, eat well and do not neglect friendships and fun. Learn to laugh at life, yourself and the enemy. Kick up your heels and enjoy the ride. Do not just watch life; live it! For Jesus' sake as well as for your own sake (and your family's), get a life.

### 2. Balance Intimacy and Warfare

What tends to happen is that one group of intercessors adopts a "bridal" mindset while another group focuses on a combative approach to prayer. The truth, however, is that the Bride of Christ wears combat boots, and the fierce warrior needs to wear a linen wedding garment. The bride needs the warrior and the warrior needs the bride. We get the idea of the "fighting Bride" from Ephesians 5:25–27 and 6:13–18, where Paul addresses first one and then the other.

As we walk with the Lord, we are meant to reach upward to hold God's hand (intimacy) while at the same time we are alert to move with God's authority outward (warfare prayer). The emphasis is never on one to the exclusion of the other. We cultivate intimacy in order to fight effectively against the powers of evil.

### 3. Watchmen and Gatekeepers Work Together

In a similar way, the watchmen on the walls (intercessory people) need to collaborate with the gatekeepers (leaders: pastors, apostles, elders, etc.). The watchmen need to report what they see, hear and discern and often they need to advise the elders as to wise strategy. Without their help, the leaders cannot defend their city successfully.

At the time the Bible was written, cities had protective walls around them, with gates. Watchmen stayed on the alert atop the walls while the city leaders conducted day-to-day business below. In time of war, the watchmen would make the call as to the trustworthiness of an approaching messenger, so that the gatekeepers could decide whether to open the gates to him—or to bar them and call forth armament.

Both groups must function as teams, not as lone rangers. The intercessory people need the protection and context of the gatekeepers. The gatekeepers must have the insights and giftings of their watchmen. Both groups need to work at breaking down barriers of mistrust that arise between them, building relational bridges of trust, serving one another with the goal of the common good of the Body of Christ.

### 4. Stick with Your Most Effective Weapons

As it is in natural war, so it is in spiritual warfare. Before you send in the ground troops, you send in the air patrol. Be wise! Bomb out the enemy's bunkers first through the weapons of high praise. Stay with it long enough to get the Holy Spirit's witness—peace, knowing, certainty—then send in the ground troops, shooting the artillery at specifically determined targets.

Praise is one of the highest weapons. Praise, like prayer, is a weapon we all can wield. Remember, God uses our praise to bind up the enemy. Psalm 149:5–9 powerfully depicts this:

> Let the godly ones exult in glory; let them sing for joy on their beds. Let the high praises of God be in their mouth, and a two-edged sword in their hand, to execute vengeance on the nations and punishment on the peoples, to bind their kings with chains and their nobles with fetters of iron, to execute on them the judgment written; this is an honor for all His godly ones. Praise the LORD!

Praise and worship release atmospheric changes. Every church and intercessory group has distinctive strengths and weaknesses, but praise-filled worship sets the stage for success. Shed your burdens at the foot of the cross and open your heart and mouth with grateful praise. Our highest moments of worship can become our most effective times of warfare as we clear the enemy out of the mid-heavens.

### 5. *Allow No Common Ground with Evil*

John 14:30 is an eye-opening verse in which Jesus is talking about His authority over the devil: "I will not speak much more with you, for the ruler of the world is coming, and he has nothing in Me." In other words, the devil has nothing in common with Jesus. And since nothing about Jesus belongs to him, he can exercise no power whatsoever over the Son of God.

Do you see the correlation? Terry Crist, in his book *Interceding against the Powers of Darkness*, casts light on this subject:

The reason Jesus was so effective in spiritual warfare . . . why He was able to confront the devil so effectively . . . in the wilderness encounter was that Jesus recognized the law of purification. The reason Jesus could stand in such power and authority and deal so effectively with the wicked oppressor of the nations was because no common ground existed between Him and His adversary. When the devil struck at Jesus, there was nothing whatsoever in Him to receive the "hit." When Satan examined Him, there was nothing for him to find. Jesus and Satan had no relationship one to another, no common ground. There was nothing in Jesus that bore witness with the works of darkness! One reason so many ministers and intercessors have been spiritually "hit" by the fiery darts of the enemy is because they have not responded to the law of purification.[1]

Let me try to explain this vital matter. Before you go chasing after external dragons and territorial spirits, make sure you hold nothing at all in common with the enemy. Let the finger of God probe into your heart, mind and actions. Open up to conviction concerning your life, family, church or ministry. Repent when necessary. Bring cleansing to your own life through the power of the blood of Jesus and yield to the work of the cross. Destroy the legal basis—the right of the enemy—to attack you. Then you can take authority over the external enemies without suffering the horrendous repercussions of inept spiritual warfare. You will have less authority over external enemies if you do not conquer them first internally.

Do not treat the name of Jesus like a magic charm or a lucky rabbit foot. Look into your own heart before you engage in spiritual warfare prayer. Sometimes believers are sincere and truly gifted, but they have common ground with the enemy. Then they prematurely wage war against the very power of darkness that has a foothold in their own lives. Let the finger of God inside you conquer your personal enemies. Then you will have assurance to defeat the spirits of wickedness in the heavenly places!

### 6. Avoid Criticizing at All Costs

Do you know what undoes intercessory groups more than anything else? It is not lack of vision, leadership or even an overt counterattack. It is the immature application of discernment expressed through criticism. This can lead to backstabbing, which left unaddressed will cause the group to splinter and the devil to win again. It all starts from subtle, simple, old-fashioned criticism. It is flat-out impossible for believers to pray together as long as they have criticism in their midst.

Once I attended an Intercessors for America conference in Washington, D.C. At one of the sessions the jealousy of the Holy Spirit came on me and I began to prophesy. I remember the word clearly:

> We are now living in the time of the coexistence of the house of David and the house of Saul. You who have been waiting, yearning, believing, longing and praying for the house of David to come forth can disqualify yourselves from being part of what you've been waiting, yearning, praying and believing for, if you sow accusation and critical speech toward the house of Saul while it yet stands. For remember, you, too, have come forth from Saul's loins.

Do you remember how David handled the "in between" time before he was elevated to the throne in place of Saul? He had opportunities, but he did not even lay a finger on his rival, Saul. Instead, he honored him.

Discernment must be stewarded carefully. We will either turn it into private intercession or gossip and slander. Criticism does not just affect the person hearing the word; when passed around, it holds back the whole community.

Avoid criticism, therefore, at all costs. As an intercessor, turn your discernment into prayer. Pray to the Father for the release of the opposite spirit (blessing) to come forth instead of criticism. Criticism does not hurt only the person who speaks it, it prevents the entire camp from moving forward. Remember what happened with Miriam when she grumbled against Moses (see Numbers 12).

### 7. *Forgiveness Is a Necessity*

Second Corinthians 2:10–11 brings us a great wisdom application for all areas of the Christian life—one that is all the more important for intercessors and leaders:

> Whom you forgive anything, I forgive also; for indeed what I have forgiven, if I have forgiven anything, I did it for your sakes in the presence of Christ, so that no advantage would be taken of us by Satan, for we are not ignorant of his schemes.

Peter wrote: "God is opposed to the proud, but gives grace to the humble" (1 Peter 5:5). When you confess your sins to another, you become a candidate to receive grace. Confession is an act of humility. The proud never confess they are wrong. They cannot see their own faults. But the humble confess their sins and thus receive grace. Healing begins to flow in and through vessels of grace. This is why James 5:16 says to "confess your sins to one another, and pray for one another so that you may be healed."

Forgiveness builds on blessing. When analysis, discerning weaknesses, accusation and criticism remain in your heart, it becomes an incubator for bitterness and unforgiveness. Instead, forgive. Release grace to a person, a church, a city, a group of people. Harboring unforgiveness in your heart is like leaving the back door wide open and giving Satan a license to carry out his strategies. Forgiveness shuts the door.

Forgiveness is not one option among others; it is an absolute necessity. I, for one, believe it is one of the most powerful weapons of spiritual warfare. The apostle Paul was saying in 2 Corinthians

2:10–11 that when we forgive, we take the advantage away from Satan. Like Paul, then, let's not be ignorant of Satan's schemes. Forgive and turn the tables on the devil. Shut the door on him and extend grace to others by walking in forgiveness.

### 8. Avoid Lures

Have you ever gone fishing? A smart fish does not bite at everything that floats by. Take trout, for example. They have keen eyesight and do not go after every lure. Trout have to be convinced that the bait is right before they will make a commitment.

Perhaps we should look to the trout to learn the lesson not to chase after every distracting lure that comes along. Lures appear unexpectedly. At times the enemy intentionally manifests his presence just to derail our pure devotion to Jesus. He is trying to capture and keep our attention. When the devil shows his head, keep your focus on Jesus.

When the devil knocks, send Jesus to answer! That might sound trite, but here is what I mean: Simply refuse to give the devil the time of day. Do not follow him! You have been called to follow Jesus. "[Fix your] eyes on Jesus, the author and perfecter of faith" (Hebrews 12:2).

This is simple but powerful. As you maintain your focus on the Lord, He releases His presence and overpowers the enemy. I am not diminishing the power of confrontational, authoritative prayer or rebuking the enemy in the name of Jesus. I am merely reminding you to choose the fights and battles you enter into. Avoid being seduced by lures. Keep your gaze fixed on Jesus, and let Him guide your use of authority.

### 9. Break the Penalty

By *break the penalty* I mean "neutralize the backlash of spiritual warfare." I used to hear this terminology in parts of the spiritual warfare camp and I did not understand it until I pulled this gem from the life of Gideon:

Gideon took ten men of his servants and did as the LORD had spoken to him; and because he was too afraid of his father's household and the men of the city to do it by day, he did it by night. When the men of the city arose early in the morning, behold, the altar of Baal was torn down, and the Asherah which was beside it was cut down, and the second bull was offered on the altar which had been built. They said to one another, "Who did this thing?" And when they searched about and inquired, they said, "Gideon the son of Joash did this thing." Then the men of the city said to Joash, "Bring out your son, that he may die, for he has torn down the altar of Baal, and indeed, he has cut down the Asherah which was beside it." But Joash said to all who stood against him, "Will you contend for Baal, or will you deliver him? Whoever will plead for him shall be put to death by morning. If he is a god, let him contend for himself, because someone has torn down his altar." Therefore on that day he named him Jerubbaal, that is to say, "Let Baal contend against him," because he had torn down his altar.

Judges 6:27–32

Here we find that a penalty—a curse or consequence—was put into place to fall on the one who would tear down the demonic high places. The Scripture does not explicitly say this, but we may infer it by the command the men of the city gave to Gideon's father: "Bring out your son, that he may die" (verse 30). Gideon's father, who owned the altar to Baal, had probably released a demonic stronghold or force to war against whoever would tear down the altar of false worship to Baal. Now he renamed his son Jerubbaal, "Let Baal contend against him" (verse 32).

Some spiritual warfare specialists inform us that professional witchcraft practitioners pronounce curses (or penalties) particularly on those who threaten their kingdom. The Old Testament picture from the life of Gideon gives us insight into the necessity of praying a hedge of protection around ourselves and our families, and breaking, in the name of Jesus, any curse or penalty that the enemy tries to enforce on God's people when they are confronting darkness.

Notice also God's reward for his valiant warriors: "The Spirit of the LORD came upon Gideon" (Judges 6:34). This means that God's Spirit *clothed* Gideon. The Holy Spirit actually took possession of him. So take heart. The reward from God can be awesome!

After engaging in a power encounter with the enemy, I have learned from experience to offer up a prayer breaking any possible counterattack that the enemy would release against me. This includes attacks against my family members, health, hope, future, calling, finances, possessions, vehicles, pets, etc. The prayer goes like this:

> *In the name of Jesus, and by the power of His blood shed on the cross, I command the penalty of the enemy, any word curse that has been pronounced against me and any backlash of the evil one sent against me and my family, to be broken. It shall not prosper as I nullify its effect in Jesus' mighty name. I proclaim a blessing to all that I am, hope to be and put my hand to, and to all that pertains to my life, health, home, finances, ministry and family. I call forth strength, vigor, protection and the supply of the Lord, for the honor and glory of His name. Amen.*

I probably did not know enough about this in my past, but now I always break the penalty in the name of Jesus and reclaim God's protection.

### 10. Whose Battle Is It?

Not every prayer battle is yours to fight. You may discern a thing, but next you need to seek God's direction. Some battles belong to you. Some belong to others. Some battles must wait for another day. Some are simply to be avoided. Never allow the devil to dictate to you when you are supposed to fight him.

I am stating this not to exaggerate the point but because I have had demonic entities stand in my bedroom and challenge me. Even when I have been forced to fight, I needed to ask for God's direction about how to do it. Paul wrote: "Thanks be to God, who always leads us in triumph in Christ, and manifests through us the sweet aroma of the knowledge of Him in every place" (2 Corinthians 2:14). He refers to the God who always leads us in triumph in Christ, which implies that we must pay attention to where and how He is leading us. Is He leading you? If you follow Him, He will give you victory. If you fail to follow Him, instead operating out of your own wisdom, you will not have His safeguards. Do not be presumptuous.

He will give you grace and protection where He has led you to go. The question becomes, "Who is leading me into this fight? Is it the Lord, strong and mighty? Is it the devil, who wants to stir me up? Is it my own unsanctified fleshly zeal?

When the Lord is leading you, you can expect victory. Intercessory battles are always His battles first and ours second. Listen carefully for His instructions.

### The Safety Net: Walking with Others

Walking with other believers constitutes an important part of wisdom for intercession. As Ecclesiastes 4:9–12 aptly remarks:

> Two are better than one because they have a good return for their labor. For if either of them falls, the one will lift up his companion. But woe to the one who falls when there is not another to lift him up. Furthermore, if two lie down together they keep warm, but how can one be warm alone? And if one

can overpower him who is alone, two can resist him. A cord of three strands is not quickly torn apart.

We all fall down occasionally for one reason or another. The Lord has wonderfully provided others to help us up when we get knocked down.

Check out another aspect of this safety net, too: "Two can resist him" (verse 12). This is an awesome promise to remember, to claim, to proclaim and to kneel on. "Five of you shall chase a hundred, and a hundred of you shall put ten thousand to flight; your enemies shall fall by the sword before you" (Leviticus 26:8 NKJV). Our power over the devil multiplies when we join with others.

Do you have a partner in prayer with whom you walk? Who is watching your back? The armor of God protects our front side, but we become one another's rear guard. Have you ever thought about that before? Let's cover one another with godly counsel, fellowship and prayer.

I am an intercessor and I have made sure that I have personal intercessors. In addition, I hold up others in prayer—always those in leadership in whatever church I belong to and also others who face daunting battles for the Kingdom, such as Mahesh Chavda, Ché Ahn, Henry and Alex Seeley, Heidi Baker and Bill Johnson. I have given myself to other ministries over the years to be an Aaron or Hur to help hold up their hands through the power of prevailing prayer (see Exodus 17:8–13). And I am grateful today for those who stand with God Encounters Ministries in our many endeavors.

The Lord can use you to help raise up "the shield of faith" (Ephesians 6:16) on behalf of others. May every ministry have its prayer shield raised up in Jesus' name!

Cry out to the Lord with me for discernment and wisdom beyond all our years. Join me, like a child, kneeling in humble adoration.

**Prayer for Wisdom in Intercession**

Lord, give me wisdom beyond my years and grant to me the spirit of wisdom and revelation in the knowledge of the glorious Lord Jesus Christ. May I be preserved by Your hand to become a veteran for the intercessors of the next generation, someone who can pass on to them treasures from Your war chest. Grateful for the opportunity to partner in Your great purposes and plans, I thank You that together we are more than conquerors in Christ Jesus. In His mighty name, Amen.

# 12

# A Heart for His Presence

*I* woke up out of a life-changing dream encounter with the Holy Spirit to find myself holding my arms out as though I were rocking a baby. Instead of humming a lullaby, I was prophesying out loud in my bedroom the same words that I had just heard in my dream: *When My people will care for, cherish, nurture and love the Bread of My Presence like a parent does his newborn child, then revival will come.* The room was charged with the tangible presence of the Lord.

In the dream, I had been holding several long loaves of bread, each wrapped in its own individual diaper-like napkin. Nestling those loaves of bread close to my heart, I had gone to find my youngest daughter's light green "blankie," which I had wrapped around the loaves and then rocked them some more.

Fully awake with my arms cradling the invisible presence of God, I prophesied those words again, now for the third time. (The first time I was still dreaming; the second time I was waking up.) The Holy Spirit really wanted me to get this. To "care for, cherish, nurture and love" the Bread of His presence may involve getting up in the wee hours of the morning with the child, holding the child close to our hearts, washing the child with love and compassion, doing simple things that make it possible for God's presence to thrive in our hearts, homes and churches.

## Homebound Watchmen

Historically, dramatic revival has come to places where intercessors have cultivated a heart for the presence of God. One of the best examples comes from the village of Barvas on the Scottish Isle of Lewis in the Outer Hebrides, off the northwest coast of mainland Scotland.

Much has been written about the impact of pastor/evangelist Duncan Campbell and the meetings he led in that time. But little attention has been paid to the prayer warriors who paved the way before and during that mighty move of God's presence. Behind the scenes labored two elderly sisters: Peggy Smith, who was 84 years old and blind, and her sister, Christine Smith, 82 years old and almost doubled over with arthritis. They were unable to attend regular church services, but for months they prayed in their home for God to send revival to Barvas. These two relentless intercessors prayed by name for the people in each cottage along their village streets. They reminded God of His Word in Isaiah 44:3: "I will pour water upon him that is thirsty, and floods upon the dry ground: I will pour my spirit upon thy seed, and my blessing upon thine offspring" (KJV). They cried out this prophetic promise to the Lord day and night. They relentlessly reminded God of His Word: "Oh that thou wouldest rend the heavens, that thou wouldest come down, that the mountains might flow down at thy presence" (Isaiah 64:1 KJV).

Across the village, independent of the Smith sisters, seven young men were meeting three nights a week in a barn to pray for revival. They had made a covenant with God and one another, according to Isaiah 62:6–7, that they would give Him no rest until He sent revival their way.[1] Month after month they labored in prayer.

One night in particular they prayed with fervency Psalm 24:3–5: "Who shall ascend into the hill of the Lord? or who shall stand in his holy place? He that hath clean hands, and a pure heart. . . . He shall receive the blessing . . . from the God of his salvation" (kjv). Instantly, it seemed, the barn was filled with the glory of God and the young men fell prostrate on the floor. An awesome awareness of God overcame them and they were drenched with supernatural power they had never known before.

At that very time, the Lord gave one of the Smith sisters a vision. Peggy Smith (who was blind, remember) saw the churches crowded with people, and hundreds being swept into the Kingdom of God. She started prophesying and proclaiming, "He's coming. He's coming. He's already here." They sent word to their pastor that they had "broken through" and that heaven was about to descend to earth.

And so it did. The whole region seemed saturated with God. Wherever people were—in the workplace, in their homes or on the roads—they were overwhelmed by the presence of almighty God. Water indeed soaked the dry ground as the conviction of the Holy Spirit was poured out in those days. A stream of blessing flowed that brought hundreds to salvation during the days of that historic visitation.[2]

The pastor in Barvas summoned a Scottish preacher named Duncan Campbell, and he is the one who gets written up in modern Church history as the revival-carrier. Seldom are the prophetic intercessors mentioned—the two elderly sisters in their cottage and the seven young men meeting in a barn.

That Hebrides Revival echoed a previous one in Wales. There, a young man named Evan Roberts prayed long and hard for revival to come to his town. When he was in his mid-twenties, he began to lead prayer services, where he taught the people to pray two simple prayers: "Send the Spirit now for Jesus Christ's sake," and "send the Spirit now more powerfully for Jesus Christ's sake." Taking turns, they would pray aloud until the presence of God came into their midst.

Then in 1904 the Spirit came powerfully to the town and surrounding region and as many as 100,000 people were brought into the Kingdom as a result; the revival sparked outpourings not only throughout Wales but also across the world.

## Open Heavens!

The term "open heavens" originates in historic revivals to describe those times when the manifest presence of God seems to bring heaven into a place in a tangible manner. Spontaneous healings take place, as well as profound conviction of sin and true conversion. It is as though a hole appears in the sky, and the celestial realm is disclosed for all to see and experience.

Ezekiel 1:1 states that "the heavens were opened and I saw visions of God." As the heavens opened, Ezekiel described a great cloud, sent by God to protect him from His brightness. Can you imagine such a sight? Then Ezekiel saw "fire [lightning] flashing forth continually" (verse 4), bright light, angels and other glorious details.

Several other Old Testament passages describe similar experiences in which the heavens parted and the heavenly came down to earth or man was somehow caught up into the heavenlies. Consider the transforming visionary experience of Isaiah: he was shown the glory of God, the fire of purification and the message of "Whom shall I send, and who will go for Us?"

(Isaiah 6:8). Likewise Daniel, as he received visions in the night, saw the Lord "like a Son of Man" coming through "the clouds of heaven" taking up His throne before the Ancient of Days (Daniel 7:13). Awesome!

Fast-forward to the New Testament. At Jesus' own baptism, as recorded in Matthew 3:16–17, "the heavens were opened" and the Holy Spirit descended on the Son of God in the form of a dove. Then the Father spoke audibly: "This is My beloved Son, in whom I am well-pleased" (verse 17).

In Acts we find Stephen, the fervent deacon, being stoned to death for preaching the Gospel. As he was dying, he saw "the heavens opened up and the Son of Man standing at the right hand of God" (Acts 7:56). The sky was loosened, the clouds were rolled back and Jesus was standing there, ready to receive him. What a sight! What a cost! But what a privilege.

John, the disciple who had laid his head on Jesus' heart at the Last Supper, had a profound experience that he recorded in the book of Revelation. John, who was by then elderly and imprisoned for his faith, was "in the Spirit on the Lord's day" (Revelation 1:10). As he meditated on his Beloved, he saw "a door standing open in heaven" (Revelation 4:1) and heard a voice calling him. He was not only able to peer into the heavenly realm, but he was also told to "come up here" (verse 1). As he did so, he saw the One who sits on the throne, with the elders, angels and four living creatures all worshiping Him in the beauty of holiness. Then John was instructed to tell the believers on earth many detailed messages from the glorified Lord Jesus Christ.

Some call open heavens "portals," "thresholds" or "gateways" in the spiritual realm. I believe there are entry points, spiritual hot spots, where God's presence becomes tangible. Remember the New Testament account about the sick people who waited at the pool of Bethesda? At certain seasons an angel of the Lord was released and stirred the water, and the first person to step into the anointed waters was healed (see John 5:1–4). Whatever you want to call them, it is my conviction that there are gateways through which God's presence seems to invade earthly space and time in a powerful way.

In the natural realm, gates are used to keep certain things out and let other things in. The elders who sit at the gates of the city (see Proverbs 31:23) are there to permit or deny entrance into their regions. So it is in the spiritual realm. Isaiah 60:18 tells us, "You will call your walls salvation, and your gates praise." We need walls of protection around every believer, family and church.

Psalm 100:4 tells us that we "enter His gates with thanksgiving and His courts with praise." Not only are we called to enter the presence of the King with thanksgiving through the gates of praise, but we are likewise expected to overtake the gateways of the enemy. Jesus said, "Upon this rock I will build My church; and the gates of Hades will not overpower it" (Matthew 16:18).

The Holy Spirit is now reopening prophetic gateways between heaven and earth. The enemy has come along, as he did in the time of Abraham and Isaac, and he has blocked up the wells of salvation with mud and refuse. Now it is time for "breakers," prophetic intercessors with a particular anointing for the purpose, to re-dig these ancient wells and allow the waters of God's healing presence to flow once again (see Genesis 26:15–22). I believe we will then move past re-digging old wells and open up entire new regions for Jesus Christ.

Today, I believe that we are now moving from an era of prophetic renewal to a new epoch of the Holy Spirit. Fueled by the prophetic prayers of watchman-intercessors, we are crossing a threshold into a time when the heavens will open over whole regions, and the brilliant presence of the Almighty will overwhelm the darkness.

## The Role of Breakers

The "breakers" are coming! These are the prophetic intercessors who help give birth to the purposes of God for their generation, and they are appearing once again. We need breakthrough in society today, but there is no breakthrough without a breaker.

Micah 2:13 describes this activity: "The breaker goes up before them; they break out, pass through the gate and go out by it. So their king goes on before them, and the LORD at their head." Truly the Lord Jesus Himself is our breaker—the One who has gone before us and broken open the gates of heaven and hell. He has done it all. But today, as in the days of John the Baptist and other strategic breakers, the Holy Spirit is looking for those who will go ahead of the pack, blaze a trail in the Spirit and open the way, that the Lord may "pass through the gate" among them.

As the young intercessors prayed David's psalm in the barn before the Hebrides Revival, so we can pray it:

> Lift up your heads, O gates, and be lifted up, O ancient doors, that the King of glory may come in! Who is the King of glory? The LORD strong and mighty, the LORD mighty in battle. Lift up your heads, O gates, and lift them up, O ancient doors, that the King of glory may come in!
>
> Psalm 24:7–9

Our prayers open the way for the King to come. They become the keys of the Kingdom that will open the gates and doors to the spiritual realm. God's angelic company often accompanies these breakthroughs, coming to our assistance as we continue to pray (see Genesis 26:15–22 and Genesis 28:10–17, for examples of angelic escorts).

Many of us are waiting for a huge word of commissioning to come, when He has already told us in His Word to love our neighbors or feed the poor right in our own backyards. I have no doubt that as we do something with the power of His presence we have already received, we will get more.

But how many of us receive words as suggestions and not commands? What are the "little" things God has commanded you to do? Did you hear these commands? Does it sound as though the Man Upstairs thinks He is God and has come to rule your life? He has. He has come to take over. The good news is that His will is good. Our little acts of kindness can be a big token of God's love to someone else.

Let's do our little stuff, then, so He can do His big stuff. May a passionate generation of violent, broken, obedient warriors arise and lay hold of the Word of God as the God of His Word lays hold of us.

It is time for the breakers to come forth for this generation, time to confront the darkness with light, time for the gatekeepers to open up the way, so that the King of glory will pass before us. It is time for the watchmen on the walls and the kingdom elders at the gates to walk together to prepare for breakthrough for this generation.

The breakers are coming to open the way. A generation of authentic, apostolic men and women, old and young, will walk in these principles and see "the knowledge of the glory of the LORD" cover the earth "as the waters cover the sea" (Habakkuk 2:14).

Right now is your heart beating a little more loudly within you as you read these lines? Do you sense Him drawing near? Is the Holy Spirit calling you to be a breaker, too?

Stop right here. Tell Him that with all that lies within you, you want Him to be honored and glorified. Volunteer to be a watchman on the walls—a prophetic intercessor. This is what you were created for. Offer yourself anew to Christ and His purposes. Do not wait. Tell Him now.

*I surrender to You, my Master and Chief. Consume me with Your Holy Spirit. Take control of my life. Make me into a prophetic intercessor who helps to make history by coming before Your throne. Put Your breaker anointing upon my life, for Your Kingdom's sake. Fill me anew, and use me. Empower me for Christ's sake. I choose by God's grace to be a watchman on the walls for my family, my city, my nation and my generation. Like Simeon and Anna, I want to see the purposes of God birthed in my life. Take possession of me, in Jesus' great name. Amen!*

## The Brilliance of His Great Presence

If you have not caught on yet, let me make one thing clear: The premier weapon of spiritual warfare is the release of God's presence. That was true when Moses led the exodus of the people of Israel from Egypt, and it is true today. Notice the importance Moses attached to God's presence:

> Then Moses said to the LORD, "See, You say to me, 'Bring up this people!' But You Yourself have not let me know whom You will send with me. Moreover, You have said, 'I have known you by name, and you have also found favor in My sight.' Now therefore, I pray You, if I have found favor in Your sight, let me know Your ways that I may know You, so that I may find favor in Your sight. Consider too, that this nation is Your people." And He said, "*My presence shall go with you*, and I will give you rest." Then he said to Him, "If *Your presence does not go* with us, do not lead us up from here. For how then can it be known that I have found favor in Your sight, I and Your people? Is it not by *Your going* with us, so that we, I and Your people, may be distinguished from all the other people who are upon the face of the earth?" The LORD said to Moses, "I will also do this thing of which you have spoken; for you have found favor in My sight and I have known you by name."
>
> Exodus 33:12–17, emphasis added

Moses interacted with God directly, and he asked, "Teach me Your ways so I might know You and so I can continue to find favor. Remember that this nation too is Your people."

God's answer addressed Moses' deepest requirements, "My presence will go with you and I will give you rest." In other words, God's Spirit would abide with Moses not only to teach him but to help him obey and lead others. The defining characteristic of the people of God, the thing that marked them as unique in all the world, was that God's presence dwelt with them. He counseled them. He gave them course-corrections. He kept them safe. He stayed with them. They were not distinguishable from others by how they dressed or how much wealth they possessed. They were not known for their loyalty to a flag or a ruler. The people of God were marked as special by the fact that the glory of God traveled with them.

As soon as Moses heard God's promise of His presence, he boldly requested: "Show me Your glory." And, with precautions, God did.

> Then Moses said, "I pray You, show me Your glory!" And He said, "I Myself will make all My goodness pass before you, and will proclaim the name of the LORD before you; and I will be gracious to whom I will be gracious, and will show compassion on whom I will show compassion." But He said, "You cannot see My face, for no man can see Me and live!" Then the LORD said, "Behold, there is a place by Me, and you shall stand there on the rock; and it will come about, while My glory is passing by, that I will put you in the cleft of the rock and cover you with My hand until I have passed by. Then I will take My hand away and you shall see My back, but My face shall not be seen."
>
> Exodus 33:18–23

God was not Moses' buddy. He was the Lord God Almighty. The glory of His presence is enough to incinerate mere mortals like us. And yet the invitation stands open to this day: *Come up here! I love you and want you to be with Me.*

Moses learned the secret: The only way to make it through the wilderness day by day and to fulfill God's heavenly call is to seek His presence daily, to tend the bread of His presence. Then every word of prayer comes into line with God's will.

Leaning in close to God's heart makes our hearts beat in unison with His. We follow Him more closely than we thought possible, saying, "Lord, to whom shall we go? You have words of eternal life" (John 6:68).

Remember, in prophetic intercession, we are not simply praying to God, we are praying with God. We are praying with God's heart!

## A Heart for His Presence—An Invitation

Father God, I desire to cultivate a heart for Your brilliant presence. Consume me with Your Holy Spirit. Take control of my life and make me into a prophetic intercessor. Fill me and empower me once again. For Your Kingdom's sake, put Your breaker anointing upon my life. I choose by God's grace to be a doorkeeper of Your presence and a watchman on the walls for my family, city and nation. Like Simeon and Anna, I want to see the purposes of God come to pass in my generation. Take possession of me, in Jesus' great name. Amen and amen!

# 21-Day Devotional Guide

*I*n this devotional designed to accompany *Praying with God's Heart,* you will find three activities for each day: *Listen, Pray* and *Obey. Listen* combines a passage of the Bible with a related excerpt from *Praying with God's Heart. Pray* supplies a prayer based on the theme of the day's reading. *Obey* provides a prompt for action. You may wish to record what the Lord speaks to you and to document how He leads you to put your prayers into action.

### ➤ *Listen*

Abraham said to his young men, "Stay here with the donkey, and I and the lad will go over there; and we will *worship* and return to you."

Genesis 22:5, emphasis added

In the Bible, the first mention of the word *worship* is found in Genesis 22, after the Lord asks Abraham to offer his son Isaac before Him on Mount Moriah. Abraham rises early the next morning, summons the young men who served under him, saddles his donkey and launches out in obedience to present his son before God. After three days of travel, Abraham's eyes rest on the site of sacrifice.

We often connect worship with music and sometimes make them synonymous. But there is no mention of music here. The only instruments listed are wood, fire and a knife, and I do not think Abraham had in mind to whittle a flute and play a tune. The scriptural account does not mention musical instruments. All he offered was sacrifice, obedience and faith. This is worship in its highest form—played on the instrument of a pure human heart.

### ➤ *Pray*

*Father God, realizing that my journey as a prophetic intercessor begins with worship, I humble myself before You, trusting You with all that is precious to me. Only You have the power to resurrect my sacrifice to bear much fruit for Your Kingdom. I worship You by laying my life down before You afresh, right now, giving You the honor that You deserve.*

### ➤ *Obey*

In your quiet time before the Lord, incorporate worship before proceeding into prayers of petition.

### ➤ *Listen*

> She came and began to bow down before Him, saying, "Lord, help me!" . . . Then Jesus said to her, "O woman, your faith is great; it shall be done for you as you wish." And her daughter was healed at once.
>
> Matthew 15:25, 28

The Syrophoenician woman had suffered a lot, but she never lost her bearings. She surrendered herself to the Lord and would not give up. She knew where her help would come from.

When you find yourself in a desperate situation, remember how prayer works. Start by offering a sacrifice of praise. Worship your way out of a victim mindset and into the presence of the Lord. "Enter into His gates with thanksgiving, and into His courts with praise" (Psalm 100:4 NKJV).

Do not be like the people who undertake a task without putting oil on their machinery. Get the oil of His anointing from its primary source—God Himself, personally. Cultivate your relationship with Him and your faith-filled prayers will flow like streams of living water.

### ➤ *Pray*

*Lord Jesus, You are my incomparable warrior, full of strength and power. I look to You for guidance and protection. I choose not to lean on my own understanding, but to look to You in all my ways. You are my Rock and the strength of my life. Quicken my spirit to be alert and watchful, to see what You are doing and follow You wholeheartedly. Give me courage for the battles that lie ahead. I want to be a part of Your army of worshipful watchers.*

### ➤ *Obey*

Cultivate intimacy in your desperation. Intimacy with the Father is an essential ingredient in fervent prayers. Ask the Lord to tenderize your heart.

### ➤ Listen

> But a Samaritan, who was on a journey, came upon him; and when
> he saw him, he felt compassion, and came to him and bandaged
> up his wounds, pouring oil and wine on them; and he put him on
> his own beast, and brought him to an inn and took care of him.

Luke 10:33–34

Latin is one of the primary languages into which the Bible
was translated hundreds of years ago, and it is from the Latin
that we get the word "intercede," which comes from *inter* ("between, among") and *cedere* ("to go, to yield or to move and to
pay a price")—in other words, "to go between." Someone who
intercedes is an intercessor, and an intercessor goes between,
steps into the gap when needed, gets involved in solving a problem. That is intercessory prayer in a nutshell.

A prayer intercessor does that in behalf of someone else,
yielding him- or herself to coming alongside in prayer those
who are weak or in need of assistance, standing in the gap
between someone and the enemy. An intercessor moves in the
direction of involvement rather than self-interest, as portrayed
in the story of the Good Samaritan.

### ➤ Pray

*Father God, put Your Spirit of grace and prayer upon me so that I can
press tenaciously through every obstacle. You are working in me to
desire what pleases You. I want to hold on to You in every situation.*

### ➤ Obey

Ask the Lord to enable you to feel His heart of compassion
so that you can get involved in solving people's problems with
Spirit-guided prayers.

### ➤ *Listen*

> Yes, truth is lacking; and he who turns aside from evil makes himself a prey. Now the LORD saw, and it was displeasing in His sight that there was no justice. And He saw that there was no man, and was astonished that there was no one to intercede.
>
> Isaiah 59:15–16

As intercessors, we stand in the gap before the Lord for those who are in great need or distress, lifting a cry to Him. He is looking for those who will do this vital duty. Join yourself to others in the Body of Christ who do not want to let God down. He is looking for people who will take up the cause. Injustices are rampant in people's personal lives, in their families, in our cities, in whole nations and people groups. By linking your heart to God's heart, you can call for justice to come forth.

### ➤ *Pray*

*Jesus, take away my heart of stone and replace it with a heart that beats with Yours. You are just and true in every way and You listen to me in the heavenly courtroom when my prayers are inspired by the perfect Advocate, Your Holy Spirit. Unite my desires to Yours so that I can stand in the gap for others who are in such deep distress that they cannot pray themselves.*

### ➤ *Obey*

Wait before God to hear from Him and to receive His pure heart of justice. Respond to Him out of that new heart.

➤ *Listen*

In the same way the Spirit also helps our weakness; for we do not know how to pray as we should, but the Spirit Himself intercedes for us with groanings too deep for words; and He who searches the hearts knows what the mind of the Spirit is, because He intercedes for the saints according to the will of God.

Romans 8:26–27

The Holy Spirit is looking for worshiping intercessors and interceding worshipers. We must learn both in order to be victorious.

Did you know that, when you have God's heart, you can be that man or that woman for your city, for your family, for your nation? God is not looking only for the one or two exceptionally zealous men or women out there, He is looking for His whole Bride, the Body of Christ, to respond to His invitation. He wants you and me to be His image-bearers. He wants our hearts to reflect His own. "Mercy triumphs over judgment" (James 2:13) and that is the goal of our intercession.

➤ *Pray*

*Holy Spirit, I do not know how to pray as I should. Help me. Thank You for the privilege of entering into the heart of Jesus. Go beyond my thoughts and words and pray through me in whatever way You choose. Release through me effective intercession that expresses Your longings and accomplishes Your will.*

➤ *Obey*

Do not pray until you have His heart, and do not settle for less than a relentless, pulsing heartbeat of persistent intercession—like His.

### ➤ *Listen*

"Shout for joy, O barren one, you who have borne no child; break forth into joyful shouting and cry aloud, you who have not travailed; for the sons of the desolate one will be more numerous than the sons of the married woman," says the LORD.

Isaiah 54:1

Travail is part of birthing in the natural as well as in prayer, but there is a kind of wrestling that often precedes the birth— the kind that faces down barrenness. The women we read about in the Bible who suffered from barrenness were desperate. They (and sometimes their husbands) prayed and agonized. And in every case, their prayers were answered with the conception and birth of a child who subsequently became a prophet or a deliverer of the nation.

### ➤ *Pray*

*Lord, deliver Your Church from barrenness and release through us the travail that brings forth life. Open the eyes of those who are blind and awaken their hearts to the knowledge of Christ. Make Your Church abundantly fruitful in the nations of the world for Your great name's sake.*

### ➤ *Obey*

If the Church would cry out like a barren woman longing for children, then we would have the revival—the new life—that is missing.

➤ *Listen*

For this reason I too, having heard of the faith in the Lord Jesus which exists among you and your love for all the saints, do not cease giving thanks for you, while making mention of you in my prayers; that the God of our Lord Jesus Christ, the Father of glory, may give to you a spirit of wisdom and of revelation in the knowledge of Him. I pray that the eyes of your heart may be enlightened, so that you will know what is the hope of His calling, what are the riches of the glory of His inheritance in the saints, and what is the surpassing greatness of His power toward us who believe.

Ephesians 1:15–19

We all have two sets of eyes: our two physical eyes and the eyes of our spirit. We believers need the eyes of our hearts open at all times. Let us pray, then, in the name of the Lord, that they will be opened up. Let's call forth the spirit of revelation into our lives.

➤ *Pray*

*Father of glory, fill me with Your Spirit of wisdom and revelation in the knowledge of Your Son, Jesus. Draw me close to Your heart so I can hear Your heart for those around me. Lord Jesus, for the sake of Your great name, release the gifts of Your Holy Spirit through me. Just as You—the Word—became flesh and dwelt among the human race, I want to be Your word in my sphere of influence so others can see Your glory and Your Kingdom advance in the earth.*

➤ *Obey*

On a regular basis, pray the prayer of Ephesians 1:15–19 for yourself. Just open your Bible and pray directly from the page.

➤ *Listen*

Now therefore, O sons, listen to me, for blessed are they who keep my ways. Heed instruction and be wise, and do not neglect it. Blessed is the man who *listens* to me, *watching* daily at my gates, *waiting* at my doorposts. For he who finds me finds life and obtains favor from the LORD.

Proverbs 8:32–35, emphasis added

These words are filled with life. Look at the three verbs used here: *listen*, *watch* and *wait*. Grasp the promises granted to those who will engage in these seemingly passive activities. It appears God uses these actions to direct us into His life.

The resulting promises:

1. You will be supernaturally blessed.
2. You will find life.
3. You will obtain favor from the Lord.

➤ *Pray*

*I often find myself in a place of unrest. I am easily distracted by things of no consequence to Your Kingdom. Help me to clear my thoughts and quiet my heart. I desire Your life and Your favor. Train me to listen, watch and wait so You can write Your revelatory words on my heart.*

➤ *Obey*

Learn to quiet your soul before God in order to commune with Him. Prayer is not so much something you do as Someone you are with.

➤ *Listen*

There was a prophetess, Anna the daughter of Phanuel, of the tribe of Asher. She was advanced in years and had lived with her husband seven years after her marriage, and then as a widow to the age of eighty-four. She never left the temple, serving night and day with fastings and prayers. At that very moment she came up and began giving thanks to God, and continued to speak of Him to all those who were looking for the redemption of Jerusalem.

Luke 2:36–38

In what way can Anna be considered a prophetess? The Scripture does not tell us that she wore a coat of camel's hair or ate locusts and wild honey. I doubt that she pointed her gnarled finger at people, declaring, "Thus saith the Lord!" and revealing the secret sins of their hearts. We have no written evidence that she ever confronted the prophets of Baal like Elijah of old or called down fire from heaven. In fact, we find not even one word of recorded prophecy from this devout woman.

If she did not give personal prophetic words, then what was her prophetic ministry? She was a woman of the secret place, not one with a public ministry at all, one who interceded with the purposes of God for her generation. The expression of her prophetic ministry was her enduring intercession. She was a prophetic, intercessory Jesus fanatic!

➤ *Pray*

*Holy Spirit, I want to be consumed by a vision of the glorious Man, Christ Jesus. Jesus, You are my goal and my prize. I want to be one who listens and watches for Your return. Give me the grace to serve You with fasting and prayer, to be a bright intercessory light all my days and to pass on a passionate torch to those who follow in my footsteps.*

## ➤ *Obey*

The Lord is searching for an "Anna Company" in our day, intercessors who will pray through the promises of the Second Coming of our Lord and Messiah. What is your response to His invitation?

➤ *Listen*

> But God . . . raised us up with Him, and seated us with Him in
> the heavenly places in Christ Jesus.
>
> Ephesians 2:4, 6

The burden of prophetic intercession begins as a flame and
grows into a consuming fire as the revelation concerning the
purposes of God for our generation increases. It might start as
an inner conviction of His will, a sudden awareness of His nearness or hearing of a situation that triggers a spiritual response.

Prayer embraces new horizons, challenges and possibilities.
It liberates intercessors from their limited human perspective.
These focused warriors now look from a heavenly vantage
point. They see with the discerning eyes of the Holy Spirit.
Their intercession assumes a revelatory dimension. As they
gather up the promises God has willed for their day and age,
they stake claim to them tenaciously in the judicial courts of
heaven.

➤ *Pray*

*Holy Father, liberate me from my limited point of view. I want
to see things from Your heavenly places and join with You to do
what is humanly impossible. I embrace the change You want to
release in the earth. Let my heart be the womb from which Your
prophetic purposes come forth. Give me the tenacity to fulfill my
role so the earth is filled with Your glory.*

➤ *Obey*

Meditate and ask what God wants you to do. Come before
Him with fresh passion to obey.

➤ *Listen*

> On your walls, O Jerusalem, I have appointed watchmen; all day and all night they will never keep silent. You who remind the LORD, take no rest for yourselves; and give Him no rest until He establishes and makes Jerusalem a praise in the earth.

> Isaiah 62:6–7

If we are up on top of the walls being watchmen, we are not down on the ground observing and participating in whatever is happening on the horizontal plane. We stay up high at our posts, because that is the only way to get an overview. As watchman-intercessors, the height of our revelation will determine our perspective.

If we watchmen on the walls will never be silent day or night, what are we saying while we are up there? We are reminding God of His Word—the promises and proclamations of Scripture as well as the current promises that are in the Father's heart today. It is as though we have been issued megaphones so that we can echo God's Word to the world around us.

➤ *Pray*

> Lord, *make me into a prophetic intercessor. Fill me anew, and use me. I choose by God's grace to be a watchman on the walls for my family, my city, my nation and my generation. Take possession of me, in Jesus' great name.*

➤ *Obey*

Volunteer to be a watchman on the walls—a prophetic intercessor. This is what you were created for.

### ➤ *Listen*

Therefore keep watch, because you do not know on what day your Lord will come. But understand this: If the owner of the house had known at what time of night the thief was coming, he would have kept watch and would not have let his house be broken into. So you also must be ready, because the Son of Man will come at an hour when you do not expect him.

Matthew 24:42–44 NIV

Our prayers open the way for the King to come. They become the keys of the Kingdom that will open the gates and doors to the spiritual realm. God's angelic company often accompanies these breakthroughs, coming to our assistance as we continue to pray.

Many of us are waiting for a huge word of commissioning to come, when He has already told us in His Word to love our neighbors or feed the poor right in our own backyards. I have no doubt that as we do something with the power of His presence we have already received, we will get more.

### ➤ *Pray*

*Jesus, I want to be eager and ready to meet You, like a passionate Bride. Wake me and infuse every tired area with Your life even as You awaken Your Church so that her lamp is burning brightly with fresh oil. Prepare us to meet You, and help us to prepare others to meet You as well.*

### ➤ *Obey*

Commit to being a prophetic intercessor who will anticipate God's desires and help thwart the enemy's efforts to defeat them.

➤ *Listen*

So faith comes from hearing, and hearing by the word of Christ.

Romans 10:17

We can believe and have faith in God because of who He is. Not only is God's Word true, but also God Himself is trustworthy. He cannot lie. When we put our whole trust in Him, we will not be disappointed. Faith makes a difference in our confidence to be able to receive and gain access to the revelatory ways of God.

Faith is a present reality. Faith is a certainty. How can we have much certainty in such an uncertain world? How can we live in a present reality of certainty while humankind exercise free will? We can have certainty because of faith. Faith is my anchor even though my boat does rock and toss on the waves of this stormy world.

Faith is so sure because it is based upon the Word of God. Consequently, our faith comes by hearing the message of the Word, the message of Christ Jesus Himself. Nothing is more absolutely certain than the Word of God.

➤ *Pray*

*Jesus, You have the words of eternal life, so I come to You to hear what You want to say. I will treasure Your Word and respond as You instruct. Stir in me greater hunger for Your Word. Help me to feed myself regularly with Your Word so that the Holy Spirit has ample ammunition to move mountains through me.*

➤ *Obey*

Have you heard any words from Jesus lately? Just read the red print in the Book and let His words sink deep into your spirit. This supplies something for the wind of God to quicken in your heart. Faith will leap up inside of you.

> *Listen*

I searched for a man among them who would build up the wall and stand in the gap before Me for the land, so that I would not destroy it.

Ezekiel 22:30

God is waiting for someone to persuade Him not to pour out His indignation. Perhaps the incense of our prayers (see Exodus 30:34–36; Psalm 141:2; Revelation 5:8; 8:3–5) will cause God's judgment to be averted or postponed. Our prayers can cut short, lessen or delay God's righteous judgments. We can use our intercessory capital to purchase seasons of mercy, to hold His judgments at bay.

> *Pray*

*Father God, You are a great and awesome God, who keeps His covenant for those who love Him and keep His commandments. Give me Your grace to stand in the gap and remind You of Your Word.*

> *Obey*

An intercessor is one who stands in the gap between God's righteous judgments and the people's need for mercy. How have your prayers done that today?

➤ *Listen*

> It came about at the seventh time, that he said, "Behold, a cloud as small as a man's hand is coming up from the sea."

> 1 Kings 18:44

God's message for us as intercessors is clear: Do not hold back!

Elijah did not only go out and declare all he had heard. He prayed the promise into being.

Before any event occurs, it must exist in the heart of God. Before the rain came to end the drought, Elijah heard the rain with his spiritual ears. Even today God speaks first.

➤ *Pray*

> *Holy Spirit, teach me to listen to You so that I can obey. And give me a tenacious spirit, one that consistently reminds You of Your Word and that gives You no rest until every word of Your Word comes to pass.*

➤ *Obey*

What has God told you to do? How are you persevering in it?

### ➤ *Listen*

Pray for the peace of Jerusalem: "May they prosper who love you. May peace be within your walls, and prosperity within your palaces." For the sake of my brothers and my friends, I will now say, "May peace be within you." For the sake of the house of the LORD our God, I will seek your good.

Psalm 122:6–9

Paul the apostle admonished the Roman church (and all believers) to pray with God's heart, writing, "Brethren, my heart's desire and prayer to God for Israel is that they may be saved" (Romans 10:1 NKJV).

Salvation comes only through our Messiah, Jesus Christ. We can say with Paul therefore: "I am not ashamed of the gospel, for it is the power of God for salvation to everyone who believes, to the Jew first and also to the Greek" (Romans 1:16).

### ➤ *Pray*

*Father God, give me the Spirit of wisdom and revelation concerning Your heart for Israel. Let Your heart for Jerusalem beat in my heart and birth Your purposes through prophetic intercession. Intercede through me until You establish and make Jerusalem a praise in the earth. Do what You long to do, Lord, for Jesus' sake!*

### ➤ *Obey*

Pray for the peace of Jerusalem. Let the Holy Spirit tune your heart to heaven.

> **Listen**

But realize this, that in the last days difficult times will come.

2 Timothy 3:1

Some years ago I took a train from Heidelberg to Rosenheim, Germany—a six-hour excursion in the middle of the night. While attempting to rest on the train, I kept hearing the gentle voice of the Holy Spirit. I know He was talking to me as an individual, but He was also imparting a burden for a band of people to come forth.

Here is what I heard Him speak:

*Where are My Daniels? Where are My Esthers? Where are My Deborahs? And where are My Josephs?*

Daniels, Esthers, Deborahs and Josephs intervene in crisis situations. They were created "for such a time as this" (Esther 4:14). Will you arise and be one of His radical prophetic intercessors? Will you be one of the answers to His persistent plea?

> **Pray**

*Father God, You have granted me authority through prayer. I cry out to You to pardon _____. They deserve Your judgment, but I ask that You relent from Your wrath against their sin. Forgive them, for they do not know what they are doing. Open their eyes. Demonstrate Your kindness and power and draw them to repentance and faith in Your Son.*

> **Obey**

Praying in tongues can result in powerful, specific revelation that aids and inspires prayerful intervention in a crisis situation.

➤ *Listen*

It is time for judgment to begin with the household of God.

1 Peter 4:17

Before you go chasing after evil spirits, make sure there is nothing you hold in common with the enemy. Let the finger of God probe into your heart, mind and actions. Open up to conviction concerning your life, family, church or ministry. Repent when necessary. Bring cleansing to your own life through the power of the blood of Jesus and yield to the work of the cross. Destroy the legal basis—the right of the enemy—to attack you. Then you can take authority over the enemy without suffering the repercussions of inept spiritual warfare.

➤ *Pray*

*Father, I want to be a person with character strong enough to house the fullness of Your power and gifts working through me. I humble myself before You and yield to the work of the cross. I turn away from my wicked ways and fix my gaze upon You.*

➤ *Obey*

Character is necessary to steward the gifts of the Spirit. Character comes only by way of the cross, and good, ripe fruit requires time exposed to the Son.

➤ *Listen*

Getting wisdom is the most important thing you can do! And with your wisdom, develop common sense and good judgment. If you exalt wisdom, she will exalt you. Hold her fast, and she will lead you to great honor; she will place a beautiful crown upon your head.

Proverbs 4:7–9 TLB

There seems to be no end to the list of things we need from God. Yet, we must learn to pray for the long haul, instead of just coming out with the occasional brilliant prayer that bursts forth like a Roman candle shooting up into the night only to fizzle out as quickly as it flared up.

Follow the example of King Solomon and request wisdom for life's journey. It is the single most vital ingredient necessary for the long haul.

➤ *Pray*

*Father God, I ask You for an impartation of Solomon-like wisdom. Show me both my strengths and my weaknesses. Capture my gaze so that my eyes remain fixed on Jesus and give me the discernment so that I can choose a wise path. Surround me with others who are wise in Your ways and enable us to support each other.*

➤ *Obey*

Ask the Lord to reveal areas of wisdom in which you are weak and to teach you what you need to know.

➤ *Listen*

> The breaker goes up before them; they break out, pass through the gate and go out by it. So their king goes on before them, and the LORD at their head.

> Micah 2:13

Truly the Lord Jesus Himself is our breaker—the One who has gone before us and broken open the gates of heaven and hell. He has done it all. But today, as in the days of John the Baptist and other strategic breakers, the Holy Spirit is looking for those who will go ahead of the pack, blaze a trail in the Spirit and open the way, that the Lord may "pass through the gate" among them.

➤ *Pray*

*Father, give me strength to be willing to break open a way for You, declaring, "Open the way that the King of glory may come in!" I ask You for a persevering spirit that seeks until it finds, that knocks until the door opens. Your Kingdom come, Your will be done, on earth in the same way as it is in heaven.*

➤ *Obey*

Our prayers open the way for the King to come. They become the keys of the Kingdom that will open the gates and doors to the spiritual realm.

➤ *Listen*

Just as the Father has loved Me, I have also loved you; abide in My love. If you keep My commandments, you will abide in My love; just as I have kept My Father's commandments and abide in His love. These things I have spoken to you so that My joy may be in you, and that your joy may be made full. This is My commandment, that you love one another, just as I have loved you.

John 15:9–12

The premier weapon of spiritual warfare is the release of God's presence. That was true when Moses led the exodus of the people of Israel from Egypt, and it is true today. Moses interacted with God directly, and he asked, "Teach me Your ways so I might know You and so I can continue to find favor" (see Exodus 33:12–17).

God's answer addressed Moses' deepest requirements, "My presence will go with you and I will give you rest." In other words, God's Spirit would abide with Moses not only to teach him but to help him obey and lead others. The defining characteristic of the people of God, the thing that marked them as unique in all the world, was that God's presence dwelt with them. He counseled them. He gave them course-corrections. He kept them safe. He stayed with them. They were not distinguishable from others by how they dressed or how much wealth they possessed. They were not known for their loyalty to a flag or a ruler. The people of God were marked as special by the fact that the glory of God traveled with them.

➤ *Pray*

*No matter how far I go into prophetic intercession, help me to stick to the basics of loving You and loving others. Amen.*

➤ *Obey*

Review the "little things" God has spoken to you during this 21-day devotional. Thank the Lord for the "wins" and take the opportunity to obey Him in areas that require more follow-up.

# Notes

### Chapter 1: The Life of Intercession: Invitation to Enter In

1. Joseph L. Garlington, *Worship: The Pattern of Things in Heaven* (Shippensburg, Pa.: Destiny Image, 1997), 5.

2. W. E. Vine, *An Expository Dictionary of New Testament Words* (Old Tappan, N.J.: Revell, 1966), 235.

3. Merriam-Webster Unabridged, s.v. "intercede."

4. Wesley L. Duewel, *Mighty Prevailing Prayer* (Grand Rapids, Mich.: Zondervan, 1990 ), 41.

### Chapter 2: Prayer Passion: Where Compassion and Passion Unite

1. R. A. Torrey, *How to Pray* (Chicago: Moody, 1900), 33–34.

2. Charles G. Finney, *Principles of Prayer* (Minneapolis: Bethany, 1980), 71.

3. William Booth quoted in Dick Eastman, *No Easy Road* (Grand Rapids, Mich.: Chosen Books, 1971), 92.

4. M. Basilea Schlink, *Repentance: The Joy-Filled Life* (Minneapolis: Bethany, 1984), 28, 33.

5. Stephen Hill, *Time to Weep: Discover the Power of Repentance That Brings Revival* (Foley, Ala.: Together in the Harvest, 1996), 237.

6. Hill, *Time to Weep*, 240.

7. Hill, *Time to Weep*, 252.

8. Duewel, *Mighty Prevailing Prayer*, 221–222.

9. Duewel, *Mighty Prevailing Prayer*, 222.

10. Vine, *Expository Dictionary*, 182.

### Chapter 3: Travail: The Prayer That Brings Birth

1. Duewel, *Mighty Prevailing Prayer*, 210–211.

2. E. M. Bounds, *The Necessity of Prayer* (Grand Rapids, Mich.: Baker, 1979), 63.

3. Leonard Ravenhill, *Why Revival Tarries* (Minneapolis: Bethany, 1982), 138.

4. Matthew Henry, *A Method for Prayer* (many editions, originally published 1710), chapter 5, "Intercession," n.p.

5. Charles G. Finney, *Lectures on Revival* (Minneapolis: Bethany, 1988), 46.

6. Quoted in Jonathan Edwards and Philip E. Howard Jr., eds., *The Life and Diary of David Brainerd* (Chicago: Moody Bible Institute, 1949, 1995), 172–173.

7. Edward Payson, *The Complete Works of Edward Payson*, vol. 1 (Harrisonburg, Va.: Sprinkle, 1846; reprint, 1987), 189.

8. Duewel, *Mighty Prevailing Prayer*, 222, citing Clara McLeister, *Men and Women of Deep Piety*, E. E. Shelhamer (Cincinnati: God's Bible School and Revivalist, 1920), 383.

## Chapter 4: Praying Down Supernatural Encounters

1. Dick Iverson, *The Holy Spirit Today: A Concise Survey of the Doctrine of the Holy Ghost* (Portland, Ore.: City Christian Publishing, 1990), 151. Some other useful definitions from other Bible teachers: "The working of miracles is the supernatural grace of God, empowering an individual to produce change that is usually perceptible and almost always instantaneous. Healings are usually gradual, where miracles are instantaneous. . . . Miracles are often triggered by a simple act of faith and obedience" (Derek Prince). "The gift of workings of miracles is a supernatural intervention in the ordinary course of nature, a temporary suspension of the accustomed order, an interruption of the system of nature as we know it, operated by the force of the Spirit" (Kenneth Hagin).

2. This occurred in 1993, as reported in "Praying Down Miracles," an article by Bruce Steinbaum that is searchable online in secondary sources.

3. C. Peter Wagner, *Warfare Prayer: How to Seek God's Power and Protection in the Battle to Build His Kingdom* (Ventura, Calif.: Regal, 1992), 21ff.

## Chapter 5: God's Heart: A Prophetic Generation

1. David Pytches, *Spiritual Gifts in the Local Church: How to Integrate Them into the Ministry of the People of God* (Minneapolis: Bethany, 1985), 79.

2. Iverson, *Holy Spirit Today*, 159.

3. R. T. Kendall, *The Anointing: Yesterday, Today, Tomorrow* (Lake Mary, Fla.: Charisma House, 2003), 2.

## Chapter 6: God's Revelatory Ways

1. James W. Goll, *Releasing Spiritual Gifts Today* (New Kensington, Penn.: Whitaker House, 2016).

2. I cover this topic much more thoroughly in my book called *The Seer* and its related study resources: James W. Goll, *The Seer: The Prophetic Power of Dreams, Visions, and Open Heavens* (Shippensburg, Penn.: Destiny Image, 2005).

## Chapter 7: Divine Insight: Praying in the Spirit

1. Sam Storms, *The Beginner's Guide to Spiritual Gifts* (Ventura, Calif.: Regal Books, 2012), 129.

2. Kenneth Hagin, *The Holy Spirit and His Gifts* (Broken Arrow, Okla.: Kenneth Hagin Ministries, 1995), 149.

3. Dick Iverson, *Holy Spirit Today*, 175.

4. Andrew Murray, *The Prayer Life* (Chicago: Moody, 1950), 35.

5. Charles G. Finney, *Sermons on Gospel Themes* (many editions).

6. Kenneth Hagin, *Why Tongues?* (Broken Arrow, Okla.: Kenneth Hagin Ministries, 1975), 31.

7. Andrew Gowers, "American Navy in Second Confrontation," *Financial Times*, 23 September 1987.

## Chapter 8: Israel: God's Prophetic Calendar

1. Tom Hess, *Let My People Go! The Struggle of the Jewish People to Return to Israel* (Washington, D.C.: Progressive Vision, 1987), 118–120.

2. Lance Lambert, *Battle for Israel* (Eastbourne, UK: Kingsway, 1975), 103.

3. Ramon Bennett, *When Day and Night Cease: A Prophetic Study of World Events and How Prophecy Concerning Israel Affects the Nations, the Church and You* (Jerusalem: Arm of Salvation, 1992), 122–123.

4. Bennett, *When Day and Night Cease*, 123.

## Chapter 9: The Power of Prophetic Intercession

1. Charles H. Spurgeon, *Spurgeon's Sermons on Prayer* (Peabody, Mass.: Hendrickson, 2007), 52.

2. See Jack Hayford, *Did God Not Spare Nineveh?* (Van Nuys, Calif.: Church On The Way, 1980).

## Chapter 10: Proclamation: Decreeing a Thing

1. Derek Prince, "By This I Overcome the Devil" in *Prayers and Proclamations* (New Kensington, Penn.: Whitaker House, 2010), 161.

## Chapter 11: Wisdom for Intercessors

1. Terry Crist, *Interceding against the Powers of Darkness* (Tulsa: Terry Crist Ministries, 1990), 19.

## Chapter 12: A Heart for His Presence

1. "On your walls, O Jerusalem, I have appointed watchmen; all day and all night they will never keep silent. You who remind the Lord, take no rest for yourselves; and give Him no rest until He establishes and makes Jerusalem a praise in the earth" (Isaiah 62:6–7).

2. This story is told in chapter 40, "The Revival in the Hebrides Islands," from the book *Revival Fire* by Wesley L. Duewel (Grand Rapids, Mich.: Zondervan, 1995), 306–318.

# Recommended Reading

*Some of these books are no longer in print, but they are readily available from internet sources.*

Alves, Elizabeth, Tommi Femrite, Karen Kaufman. *Intercessors: Discover Your Prayer Power.*

Bennet, Ramon. *When Day and Night Cease: A Prophetic Study of World Events and How Prophecy Concerning Israel Affects the Church and You.*

Bickle, Mike. *Growing in Prayer: A Real-Life Guide to Talking with God.*

———. *Passion for Jesus: Cultivating Extravagant Love for God.*

Bounds, Edward McKendree. *The Complete Works of E. M. Bounds on Prayer.*

Chavda, Mahesh. *Only Love Can Make a Miracle: When God's Power Takes Hold of a Man, It Can Shake the World.*

Chavda, Mahesh, and Bonnie Chavda. *The Watch of the Lord: The Secret Weapon of the Last-Day Church.*

Cooke, Graham. *Developing Your Prophetic Gifting.*

Cornwall, Judson. *Praying the Scriptures: Communicating with God in His Own Words.*

Duewel, Wesley. *Mighty Prevailing Prayer: Experiencing the Power of Answered Prayer.*

———. *Revival Fire.*

Eastman, Dick. *Love on Its Knees: Make a Difference by Praying for Others.*

Engle, Lou. *Digging the Wells of Revival: Reclaiming Your Historic Inheritance through Prophetic Intercession.*

Finto, Don. *Your People Shall Be My People: How Israel, the Jews and the Christian Church Will Come Together in the Last Days.*

Foster, Richard J. *Prayer: Finding the Heart's True Home.*

Frangipane, Francis. *This Day We Fight! Breaking the Bondage of a Passive Spirit.*

Goll, James W. *The Coming Israel Awakening: Gazing Into the Future of the Jewish People and the Church.*

———. *The Discerner: Hearing, Confirming, and Acting on Prophetic Revelation.*

———. *Empowered Prayer: 365-Day Personal Prayer Guide.*

———. *Hearing God's Voice Today: Practical Help for Listening to Him and Recognizing His Voice.*

———. *Intercession: The Power and Passion to Shape History.*

———. *The Lifestyle of a Watchman: A 21-Day Journey to Becoming a Guardian in Prayer.*

———. *The Lifestyle of a Prophet: A 21-Day Journey to Embracing Your Calling.*

———. *The Lost Art of Intercession.*

———. *The Lost Art of Practicing His Presence.*

———. *Passionate Pursuit: Getting to Know God and His Word.*

———. *Prayer Storm: The Hour That Changes the World.*

———. *Releasing Spiritual Gifts Today.*

———. *The Seer: The Prophetic Power of Visions, Dreams, and Open Heavens.*

Goll, James W. and Michal Ann Goll. *Dream Language: The Prophetic Power of Dreams, Revelations, and the Spirit of Wisdom.*

Goll, James W. and Lou Engle. *The Call of the Elijah Revolution: The Passion for Radical Change.*

Grubb, Norman. *Rees Howells, Intercessor: The Story of a Life Lived for God.*

Hess, Tom. *The Watchmen: Being Prepared and Preparing the Way for Messiah.*

Hill, Stephen. *A Time to Weep: Discover the Power of Repentance That Brings Revival.*

Jackson, Harry, Jr. *The Way of the Warrior: How to Fulfill Life's Most Difficult Assignments.*

Jacobs, Cindy. *Possessing the Gates of the Enemy: A Training Manual for Militant Intercession.*

———. *The Voice of God: How God Speaks Personally and Corporately to His Children Today.*

Joyner, Rick. *The Prophetic Ministry.*

Kendall, R. T. *The Anointing: Yesterday, Today and Tomorrow.*

Petrie, Alistair. *Releasing Heaven on Earth: God's Principles for Restoring the Land.*

Pierce, Chuck, and John Dickson. *The Worship Warrior: Ascending in Worship, Descending in War.*

Prince, Derek. *Promised Land: The Future of Israel Revealed in Prophecy.*

———. *Shaping History through Prayer and Fasting: How Christians Can Change World Events through the Simple Yet Powerful Tools of Prayer and Fasting.*

Ruscoe, Doris. *The Intercession of Rees Howells.*

Sheets, Dutch. *Authority in Prayer: Praying with Power and Purpose.*

———. *Intercessory Prayer: How God Can Use Your Prayers to Move Heaven and Earth.*

Wentroble, Barbara. *Prophetic Intercession: Unlocking Miracles and Releasing the Blessings of God.*

Wimber, John, and Kevin Springer. *Power Healing.*

# General Index

# Scripture Index

## Old Testament

### Genesis

2:7 153
6:8 102
11:30 61, 62
17:4–8 131
18:1–15 61
18:9–14 62
18:20–21, 23–32 155–156
20:7 22
21:1–3 62
21:1–8 61
22 22, 205
22:5 22, 205
25:21–22, 24 63
25:21–26 61
26:15–22 200, 201
28:10–17 201
29:31 61, 63
30:1, 22–24 61
30:22–24 63
32:24–26 54
35:16–18 61

### Exodus

2:23–25 60
17:8–13 192
30:34–36 28, 222

33:8–11 97
33:12–17 203, 229
33:18–23 204

### Leviticus

Book of 117
26:8 192

### Numbers

6:24–26 104
11:14 89
11:16–17 89
11:25 89
11:26–29 90
11:27 91
11:28 91
11:29 91
12 187
23:19 109

### Deuteronomy

13 112
28:2, 4, 11 33
32:3–4 168

### Joshua

6 175
6:10 175

### Judges

6:6–7 60
6:11–14 175
6:27–32 189
6:30 189
6:32 189
6:34 190
13:2–6, 8–9, 15–20, 24
   63–64
13:2–24 61

### Ruth

4:13 61

### 1 Samuel

1:2–20 61
1:4–5, 9–18, 19–20 64–65
7:9 60
17:43–51 173–174
17:45–47 174

### 1 Kings

18:41–46 68–70
18:44 223

### 1 Chronicles

5:20 60

247

**James W. Goll** is a lover of Jesus and founder of God Encounters Ministries, which is dedicated to releasing God's presence through equipping and discipling materials on the prophetic, prayer and the presence of God.

James has traveled extensively to over fifty nations, carrying a passion for Jesus wherever he goes. He is a member of the Harvest International Ministry apostolic team and a consultant to leaders and ministries around the world. James desires to see the Body of Christ become the house of prayer for all nations and be empowered by the Holy Spirit to spread the Good News of Jesus to every country and to all peoples.

James and Michal Ann Goll were married for more than 32 years before her graduation to heaven in the fall of 2008. They have four wonderful adult children, all of whom are now married; and James is now "Gramps" to a growing number of grandchildren. He makes his home in Franklin, Tennessee.

### For More Information

James W. Goll
God Encounters Ministries
P.O. Box 1653
Franklin, TN 37065
Phone: 1-877-200-1604

www.godencounters.com

info@godencounters.com
cs@godencounters.com • classes@godencounters.com

Facebook, Instagram, Twitter, GEM Media,
XP Media, Kingdom Flame,
YouTube, Vimeo, Charisma blogs, iTunes podcasts

# More from James W. Goll

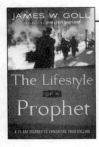

This unique, hands-on 21-day guide helps all believers develop intimacy with God so they can hear His voice clearly—and then proclaim His words faithfully. This is a must-have resource for those in prophetic ministry and all who work with them.

*The Lifestyle of a Prophet*

Bestselling author James Goll takes you on an adventure into the heart of what it means to hear God, and how to do it. On this journey, both beginners and those who have been listening to God for years will explore biblical principles about prayer, starting from square one. Let this be the start of a lifestyle of hearing God in your daily life!

*Hearing God's Voice Today*